M.34
Y

C0-DVE-772

FIC   89-0482
HER   Hermes, Patricia
                 W   ll take
              ca   e of m ?

DATE DUE

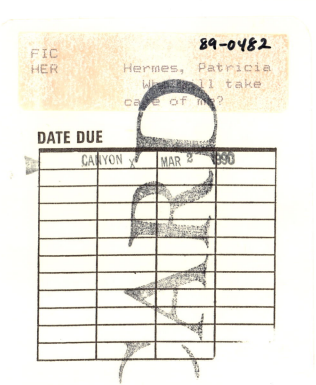

	CANYON x	MAR 2 890	

WHO WILL TAKE CARE OF ME?

Patricia Hermes

WHO WILL TAKE CARE OF ME?

Shasta County Office of Education
Instructional Materials Center
1644 Magnolia Avenue
Redding CA 96001-1599

Harcourt Brace Jovanovich, Publishers

San Diego   New York   London

89-0482

Copyright © 1983 by Patricia Hermes

All rights reserved. No part of this publication may be reproduced or transmitted in any form or by any means, electronic or mechanical, including photocopy, recording, or any information storage and retrieval system, without permission in writing from the publisher.

Requests for permission to make copies of any part of the work should be mailed to Permissions, Harcourt Brace Jovanovich, Publishers, Orlando, Florida 32887

Printed in the United States of America

Library of Congress Cataloging in Publication Data

Hermes, Patricia.
  Who will take care of me?

  Summary: Terrified that the death of the grandmother who was their guardian will separate them, twelve-year-old Mark decides to run away with his retarded younger brother.
  [1. Brothers—Fiction. 2. Mentally handicapped—Fiction. 3. Orphans—Fiction] I. Title.
PZ7.H4317Who 1983   [Fic]   82–48757
ISBN 0–15–296265–4

C D E

Again for my family—
And for Margaret "Bunny" Gabel
with gratitude

WHO WILL TAKE CARE OF ME?

I

The hill angled away from Mark, the way the little windows in his room did when he pushed them up and out to let in a breeze on hot summer days like this one. The angle was so sharp that it made him catch his breath in fear. But it was too late to stop now, even had he wanted to—and he didn't want to. It had been his idea to race down the hill ever since he and his brother, Pete, found the rusty old wagon in the garage, and Pete, so willing to do anything with him, had joined in immediately.

Mark turned to Pete. "Ready."

"Go!" Pete shouted. "Go, go, go!"

Mark was off—racing downhill in the wagon, racing for no reason but the fun of it, racing as he had never raced before. Keeping a knee in the wagon, he pumped hard with the other leg, harder and faster, the way Grandma had taught him to do when he was very little. It began to come back to him now how to do it—pump, pump, harder and faster.

The wind whistled by him, catching his breath and tearing it away, ballooning up the sleeves of his shirt so he felt as though he'd be airborne at any minute. Trees sped up to him, blurred as he passed, and then disappeared.

He threw back his head and shouted for pure joy. "Aaah!" Then he pretended he was afraid and screamed, "Aiii!"—the way people do at horror movies. He screamed because out here, where he lived, no one could hear him—no one perhaps but the crows circling in the sky, or the cows that he rushed past, or Pete, who was back at the top of the hill.

He pumped harder and faster and felt tears in his eyes as the wind made them sting and smart. The hill began slackening out before him, the tilt not quite so sharp now, tapering slowly. In a while, the wheels of the wagon, rusty from disuse, slowed as they bumped over the ground.

His breath began to come back, first in gasps, then in a more normal, slower rhythm.

With the tip of his sneaker, he ground himself to a halt. He got out of the wagon, turned, and looked back up the hill. There were two people there now, Pete and . . . who? Like scarecrows they stood silhouetted against the sky. Poor, dumb old Pete. Poor, lovable old Pete. Ten years old with the mind of a little kid, of a five-year-old, maybe. But who was with him? Was it . . . ohmigosh, it was. Grandma! How had she come to be there? Probably heard him shouting. He had been dumb to do that. They lived only a few hundred yards from the top of the hill, and she had probably thought he was being murdered or that something had happened to Pete. Was she going to be mad that he had raced down here like a maniac? Or mad that he had left Pete alone for a minute?

He squinted but couldn't see the expression on her face. He couldn't see Pete's expression either, but it was clear that he was excited. He stood there waving his arms like a windmill, so that if anyone were near, Pete would have knocked him flat. "Me too, me too!" Pete was shouting. Mark couldn't hear the words, but he smiled, knowing that was what Pete was saying. Those were among his favorite words, those and "looka'."

As Mark pulled the wagon up the hill, Grandma's figure seemed to grow in size. She was small, only about as big as Mark, and from where he stood, she looked like a friendly little witch as she leaned on a rake handle and the wind flapped her big sleeves. She used a cane about the house, but lately, as she worked in her garden or walked around outside, she had begun carrying a broken-off rake handle for support. She said it steadied her and gave her more confidence.

When he reached the top of the hill, Grandma tapped the face of her watch. "Forty-two seconds," she said solemnly. "One of the fastest times on this hill."

"Faster than when you were little?"

"Not that fast."

"Want a turn?"

"Tomorrow," she answered.

He laughed, relieved. She was fooling! She wasn't mad.

"Me! Me!" Pete was yanking at the wagon handle, trying to snatch it from Mark's hold. "Me go!"

"Hold your horses!" Mark glared at him.

Pete made a face, jutted out his lower lip, then folded his arms and turned his back.

Mark laughed and patted Pete's back. "Come on. I'll take you." He looked at Grandma. "Okay if I go with him?"

Grandma nodded, then turned to Pete. "You can go, but Mark's going with you."

"No!" Pete turned around, jutted out his lip again, and glared at Grandma. "No!" He shouted it so loud that even Mark, who was used to Pete's shouts, jumped.

Grandma shook her head. She reached over to Pete and put one finger gently across his lips. "Shhh!" she whispered. She drew the sound out in a long, slow way and smiled at him. As Mark watched, an old, familiar sadness swept over him. Sadness, or was it jealousy? Grandma was so nice to Pete. She loved him—Mark, too. He knew that, but still he felt left out sometimes.

Grandma's finger was still on Pete's lip, and Pete made a snapping motion with his mouth, as though to bite her fingers, but he pulled away. "Okay," he whispered.

He turned to Mark. "Go?" he whispered, and he sounded like a very little boy.

Mark nodded and showed him how to get into the wagon. Pete had forgotten to argue by then and allowed Mark to help him. When Pete was wedged into the front, his feet encircling the wagon handle, Mark got in behind. There was barely room, just enough for his knee, and he had to reach around Pete to hold the handle.

"Ready?" he said.

"Go!" Pete demanded.

Like a freight train, they lumbered away from the top of the hill, the weight of the two of them almost too much to get the wagon moving. Mark grunted as he tried to push. They inched their way to the top of the incline and then to the crest of the hill. Where it tipped away steeply, they began to pick up speed.

"Go! Go!" Pete shouted.

Mark kept one foot near the ground, dragging it occasionally to keep them from going out of control. Trees rushed by again, faster than before, blurs of green and brown. A flock of birds, flushed from the grass, flew up in alarm, and the crows above began calling crazily. "Ha, ha, ha!" Mark imagined them saying.

"Go! Go!" Pete was shouting. He turned to look at Mark, his eyes wide, and the wagon tipped wildly.

"Oh, no!" Mark screamed. All their weight was against his extended foot. Pain tore through the leg, and it felt as though it would snap. He gritted his teeth, flung his body to the far side, and after a pause that seemed to go on forever, the wagon righted itself.

His heart was thumping wildly, but gradually his breathing became more regular.

They were at the foot of the hill, the wagon bumping with hard, little knocks against stones and ruts. They crunched to a halt, and Mark climbed out. Never—never again would he do that! He wouldn't stop shaking for a week. He looked at Pete, but Pete was smiling happily, breathing hard and grinning as though he had just gotten off a roller coaster.

"Did you like it?" Mark asked.

"Yeah!" Pete shouted, and Mark winced.

They began the long walk back to the top of the

hill, Pete walking ahead and pulling the wagon behind him. Suddenly he stopped. "Oh, Mark, looka'!" It was the tone of voice he reserved only for animals —soft and full of wonder.

Mark looked in the direction in which Pete pointed. There was a squirrel sitting atop a fence, its bushy gray tail flicking slowly back and forth as it kept its balance. It was just a regular, ordinary squirrel, but Pete's face was lit up as though he had found a treasure.

He turned to Mark, a "May I?" look on his face, and Mark nodded. He knew Pete would try to pet the squirrel, the way he tried to touch every animal. It never worked. The animals always ran away before Pete could reach them, but Mark had learned to wait while Pete tried.

Carefully, Pete set down the handle of the wagon. His lower lip was caught between his teeth. He crept forward softly, as though he weighed nothing, as though he were a feather or a breeze. Without a sound, he moved toward this soft gray creature whose tail switched silently.

But though Pete moved quietly, the squirrel sensed his presence. It watched him come, its brown, round eyes bulging. Then, with a careless flick of its tail, it bounded from the fence onto the trunk of a tree and quickly disappeared up into the leafy branches.

Pete turned, tears forming in his eyes and his lower lip trembling.

Mark smiled, then came up and took his brother's hand. "Come on," he said. "It's okay, buddy." He picked up the handle of the wagon and tugged at Pete.

Pete's lip was still thrust out, and he gave Mark

one of those looks out of the corner of his eye that always made Mark laugh. It wasn't that he didn't sympathize with Pete. It was just that it always ended the same way, and Pete never learned.

"Come on, Pete," Mark said again. "Let's go home, and then you can see the ducks." There were ducks in the pond at home, and some of them had become so tame that once in a while Pete was able to pat them.

"Ducks!" Pete exclaimed, and immediately began trudging along beside Mark.

At the top of the hill, Grandma was sitting on the curb, the rake handle across her knees. "You scared me half to death," she said.

"I scared *me* half to death," Mark answered. "How fast did I go?"

"Too fast. I don't think we'll do that again, will we?"

Mark shook his head.

"Help me up?" she asked.

Mark braced himself, held out both hands, and took Grandma's hands in his. No matter how many times he did this—and Grandma had needed help for a long time now—Mark was always surprised by the softness of her hands. It wasn't just the skin. The whole hand was soft, as though there weren't any bones, as though they were made of fluff or something. Yet Grandma was strong—he knew that— very strong for her age. How old was she? He wasn't sure, but he knew she was over eighty.

With a small tug, he had her on her feet, and she smiled her thanks at him. For a moment she stood there, wiping the seat of her pants with one hand, then smoothing her hair with the other. He handed her the rake handle, and she fussed with it for a minute, turning it this way and that, as though look-ing for a proper grip. It struck him after a minute that she was stalling, that something was wrong. He watched her carefully. She seemed out of breath again, the way she had been several times recently. Particularly in the mornings, he had noticed that it seemed to take a long time for her to get started, as though she had to organize everything first, even her breathing.

Now ready, she walked away, stepping strongly in spite of her previous hesitation, but holding the stick for support.

Mark turned to Pete. Where was he? "Pete! Peter!" he called. He could hear the fear in his own voice.

"Here!" Pete shouted.

He was by the fence where the squirrel had been, staring morosely into the woods. "Ready?" Mark said. "Ready to go see the ducks?"

Pete nodded vigorously, raising his head way up and then lowering it way down—extremes, the way he did everything. Then suddenly, for no apparent reason, he came and hugged Mark, squeezing him fiercely, almost taking Mark's breath away, and rocking him back and forth.

Mark let himself be hugged, and he grinned over Pete's shoulder and patted his back. "You're a good kid, Pete," he whispered. "You're one good kid."

II

When they got home, Grandma went directly to her garden and Pete to the duck pond, but the ducks were so far out in the water that he could only stare at them longingly. He had named each one, and now he called them by name. To Mark, they all looked alike. Oh, some were bigger than others, but other than that, they were identical. Only Pete would know the difference. Funny. Pete didn't understand so many things, and he had to be watched like a little child; yet he was smart about some things. It didn't surprise Mark at all that Pete knew which duck was which.

"Hey, Pete?" Mark called, after watching him for a minute. "What're you doing?"

"Ducking."

"What?"

"Ducking!" Pete shouted.

"Shush! You're hurting my ears!" Mark shouted back.

"Am not!" Pete replied.

Mark laughed. *Ducking?* He sat down on the porch steps, rubbing his toe around in the dirt. Summer had to be the most boring time in the whole world, especially when you had a brother like Pete. All you could do was stay home and watch him and care for him. Pete could hardly do anything for himself. Only last week had he finally learned to do buttons. And it seemed as though he would never be able to talk like everybody else. Whenever he learned a new word, he said it over and over again— *shouted* it. Grandma was always putting one finger over his lips. "Shush," she would say softly. And then, for about two minutes, Pete would talk like everybody else.

Mark sighed. Nothing to do but watch Pete. If only there were someone around who would come over, someone to play with while he watched Pete. In his mind he went over the list of the few friends he had. David was at camp. Jeff was at camp. Elliott was at his cottage at the lake. Morris? He wouldn't play with Morris in a million years unless he was the only one left in town. And now, not even Morris was left.

If only Grandma would open their cottage at the lake! It wasn't a fancy place, just a little three-room cabin, but both Mark and Pete loved to go there. But Grandma said it was still too cold. Cold for her, maybe. Not for him. Mark loved the lake in June.

If Grandma would watch Pete for a while, he could get on his bike and go somewhere, into town perhaps to look in the sports store. There had to be *something* to do besides watch Pete. He stood up. "Grandma?" he called.

She was bent over, picking tomatoes, and she looked up at the sound of his voice. She smiled at him, that instant smile she got whenever she saw him, and he felt a warm feeling spread over him, just as suddenly as the sadness had swept over him before. He smiled back. "Can I go somewhere?"

"Where?"

"Don't know. Just somewhere."

She nodded and straightened up, putting one hand to her back as she did. "I'll be right there, and then you can go. Come, bring some of these tomatoes in for me."

He went to her. She had picked about a thousand tomatoes, all of them warm and sandy and ripe. He lifted the basket and found it weighed about a ton. "What are you going to do with all of these?"

"Make tomato brownies," she said solemnly.

He shuddered, and she laughed and winked at him. Then she laid one hand on his shoulder and, balancing herself with the rake handle on the other side, walked slowly to the house.

At the porch, Mark set down the basket. As he straightened up, he found that Grandma was looking at him. "You are a very nice person," she said slowly. "A very, very nice person."

Her saying that surprised him. She so seldom said things like that, and he didn't know what he had done to cause it. He looked away. "You're pretty nice, too," he said after a second. He nodded toward Peter, trying to change the subject. "He's going to have a fit when I leave."

"You leave Peter to me," she said. She called to Pete then. "Come here, Peter."

He came, walking slowly, his feet flapping in that funny way of his, as though they were loose, hardly attached to his legs. Grandma put a hand on his arm, and together they went into the house.

Mark went up the steps after them and closed the screen door behind them. "See you later, Grandma," he said. "See ya, Pete."

"Where you going?" Pete shouted.

"Out."

"Me too!"

"No!" Mark glared at him. "Not this time."

"Yes." Pete put his little round face up to the screen door and pushed out his lip. "Yes, yes, yes."

"No, no, no."

"Now stop it, you two," Grandma said. "Peter, come here. You can help me. I'm going to make something for you."

Pete turned away from the door, and the minute his attention was elsewhere, Mark went down the steps, got his bike, and went out of the yard. He closed the gate tightly behind him, latching it on the outside, because Pete couldn't be trusted not to disappear. Not that he deliberately ran away, but it was so easy for Pete to get lost, even if he was only a block away from home. Mark remembered the night last summer when Pete had disappeared for an hour. Everybody in the neighborhood, all the families, had gone looking. Mark could still remember the fear in Grandma's voice as she called his name. They had found him that night in the churchyard, sitting on the steps, sound asleep. He was just one block from home.

Mark remembered that night as sad, not just because Pete was lost, but because all the mothers and fathers in the neighborhood had been out looking together. He had wished that night, for the first time in a very long time, that he had a mother and father too. Most of the time he just accepted the fact that other kids had mothers and he had a grandmother. He knew that both his parents had died in an accident. Grandma had often told him the story, but it had happened when he was too young to remember. Since he had never known them, he never missed them. But that night, and lots of other nights since, he had dreamed of having real parents.

Now, with the gate fastened tightly behind him, Mark got on his bike and pedaled down the road to town. The slight breeze from the movement of the bike felt good on his face, and he tipped his head back for a moment. About a mile down the road, he passed the school, deserted now and silent, as though it were sleeping. In a little over two months it would be so different—windows open, the noise of kids inside, and yellow buses parked outside. He smiled. He had to be the only person in the world who longed for school to start. Of course, he'd never admit that to anyone, or people would think him weird. But he did like school. For one thing, it was his only chance to get away from Pete, but besides, he really did like studying and learning new things.

He bicycled across town, not seeing anyone along the dusty road. Once, a farmer off in a field waved to him, and he saw a dusty, sleepy dog, but other than that, there was no one. It was as though the entire town had gone to sleep. He passed the sporting-goods store, slowed, but decided against stopping. No sense, when you didn't have any money. He thought of stopping when he reached Aunt Agnes's house, but decided against that, too. He liked Aunt Agnes, loved her, probably, but sometimes she talked nonstop and got on his nerves.

At the far side of town, he came to Dr. Ramirez's house, and there he slowed. Dr. Ramirez was a friend, and he'd taken care of Mark and Pete for as long as Mark could remember. He took care of Grandma, too, and many nights he'd come and sit on the porch swing and talk. Sometimes he and Mark would play checkers. Mark stopped his bike, then got off, standing for a moment and looking at the house. He had often stood and looked at this house, trying to figure out why it seemed different from others in this town. It wasn't any bigger or fancier. It had a porch running around all sides as they did, and there were plants on it, as there were on the others. But small things, like the plants, made it seem different. Most people's plants were set in tin cans, the kind that juice or motor oil came in. People peeled off the labels and used the cans as planters for little yellow marigolds or hard, green, rubbery spikes of something or other. At Dr. Ramirez's house, all the plants were in big, wicker baskets, clustered together as though an entire garden had sprung up in one spot. They weren't the small, rubbery things, but big sweeping ferns and tall, leafy trees.

Other things were different, too. There was a round table on the porch with a small blue rug under it and two wicker chairs beside it. Many afternoons Mark had played checkers with Dr. Ramirez there. Mark smiled, looking at it all, remembering what Grandma had said about this porch, that it was hard to believe it was the home of a bachelor, that it had a "woman's touch."

Mark set his bike down at the curb, then went up and rang the bell. The inner door was open, and through the screen he could hear the bell peal through the house, tinkling softly like a wind chime. In a moment, footsteps could be heard, and then someone crossed the hallway, blocking out the light from inside.

"Hey, Mark!" Dr. Ramirez threw the door open, and his hearty voice seemed to fill the inner hallway. He stepped out onto the sunlit porch and took Mark's hand, shaking it as though he hadn't seen Mark in a year. It was the way he always greeted Mark, warmly, as though he were really glad to see him.

He motioned Mark to a chair by the table, then sat down facing him, his curly shock of gray hair framing his tanned, lined face. "What's doing?"

Mark shrugged. "Nothing."

Dr. Ramirez eyed him quizzically. "Anything wrong at your house?"

Mark shook his head. "Nope. Bored though."

The doctor nodded. "Summers are like that. How about a little checkers?"

"Sure. But I'll beat you."

"Want to bet?"

"Yeah. How much?" This was their usual routine, and Mark smiled.

Dr. Ramirez laughed. "No money. I don't have any. We'll trade for services today. I win, you cut that lawn." He nodded toward the front.

"*I* win," Mark said instantly, "you get Peter for an entire day." He shook his head then, reconsidering. A whole day was too much to ask of anyone. "For an afternoon," he said.

Again Dr. Ramirez laughed. "He's getting to you, eh?"

"Uh-huh."

"Okay, it's a deal."

Dr. Ramirez pulled the checkerboard out from the lower shelf of the table, and they both bent eagerly over the game. This time Mark was no match for the doctor. In about five minutes he had been wiped out, all of his pieces cleaned neatly from the board.

Dr. Ramirez stood up, wiped his hands on his pants, and grinned. "I'll get you some lemonade. You get the lawn mower out."

Mark made a face, but he got up and went to the garage, where he knew the mower was kept. He had often mowed the lawn for the doctor as a favor or sometimes just to have something to do. He didn't really mind today. There was nothing to do anyway.

By the time the lawn was finished, he was sweating like mad and had finished about half a gallon of the lemonade the doctor had made for him. He went up the steps and wiped his face with the hem of his shirt. He leaned back against the house just as the doctor came out, his black bag in his hand. He was hurrying. He stuffed something in Mark's pocket as he went by. "Got a call to make," he said. "That's for you."

Puzzled, Mark reached into his shirt pocket, took out a crumpled-up bill, and unfolded it. Five dollars! He looked up. He couldn't accept that.

As if reading his thoughts, Dr. Ramirez called from the driveway, "Take it! And you don't have to tell your grandma about it, either. I owe it to you."

"But I can't!"

"Yes you can. Just keep your big mouth shut." He got into the car and waved to Mark. "Buy something good. See you."

Mark stood up, stuffed the bill deep into the pocket of his pants, and called back, "See you." Then he added softly, "Thanks."

III

A whole month later, the five-dollar bill still lay in a small tin box in the top drawer of Mark's dresser. He had not had time to spend it, nor did he have time even to think about it. He had been too busy and too worried. For weeks, Grandma had been ill and seemed to become worse as each day went by. Mark's time was completely taken up with caring for Peter and preparing meals. Aunt Agnes came almost every day to help, but still the responsibility for Pete fell almost entirely on Mark.

But how could Grandma get sick so fast? She was old—he knew that—but she was strong, too, or used to be. Now she was in bed much of the time. Hardly a day went by that Dr. Ramirez didn't come to check on her. After he came out of her room, his face always had a deep, worried frown. Even when he sat with Mark on the porch afterward and talked, he seemed preoccupied. There had not even been a checker game since that day early in the summer.

It was midday now on the hottest day of the summer so far. Dr. Ramirez was inside with Grandma, and Mark sat on the steps praying, his eyes squeezed shut. He listened for sounds from the house behind him, but everything was still. He could hear only the sound of Grandma's heavy breathing—a loud, whistling breath, then a pause, then another loud breath and another pause, even longer this time. Mark held his own breath while he listened. "Breathe, Grandma, breathe," he prayed silently. "Please!" After what seemed forever, there was a raspy, choking cough and a sort of sigh. Then he could hear her breathing again, in and out.

Mark took a deep breath and looked down the yard to where Pete was playing. Oh, no! Mark jumped up. "Get out of there! Right now!" he shouted. Pete was in the pond, a pond so dirty that even the ducks seemed to avoid it except on the hottest days. "Get out, Pete. Now!"

Pete looked up at him and grinned. "Okay, okay!" he shouted. It was Pete's newest favorite word. "Looka', Mark, looka'!"

Pete backed out of the pond. After a quick look over his shoulder to be sure his brother was still watching, he turned and took a running leap at the pond, belly-whopping into it, his small, hard middle slapping against the water.

Mark couldn't help laughing. "Okay, Pete," he called. "But no more. Remember what Grandma said? That water's too dirty to be in."

Even from that far away, he could see Pete's face

light up. "Grandma?" Pete said hopefully. He came up the sloping yard to the steps, his feet flapping, and stood in front of Mark. "Grandma?"

"No." Mark shook his head. "Can't see Grandma yet. Dr. Ramirez is with her."

Pete nodded slowly. For a minute his eyes were clear, as if he understood.

"Oh, if only you did understand!" Mark thought. "What am I going to do with you? Who will take care of you if Grandma . . . dies?" Even thinking that word made Mark shiver, as if the sun had just gone in. After all, he was twelve years old, hardly a baby, but he couldn't really take care of Peter alone. Who would take care of them? Would Aunt Agnes come to live with them?

These thoughts ran around in his mind, the way they had ever since Grandma got so ill. It had happened before, he and Peter being left alone, but he had been too little to remember it. Grandma had told him about it frequently enough, about the accident and how his mom and dad and grandpa had all died. Grandma would sit on the porch swing— Mark on one side of her and Peter on the other, with the photo album on her lap——showing them pictures of their mom and dad. Then she'd tell them how much their parents had loved them and hadn't wanted to leave them. But when she finished the story, she would tell them over and over not to worry, that she would take care of them always. That's what she said. Always.

Mark looked into Pete's eyes now. Pete still had that quiet, waiting expression. Lightly, playfully, Mark punched Pete's arm. "Hey! Smile!" He grinned and wondered if his brother knew how fake the smile really was. "Can't see Grandma yet. But maybe later, okay?"

Pete nodded but didn't punch back as he usually did. His lower lip came out, and tears shimmered in his eyes. "Why, you understand, don't you?" Mark thought suddenly. "You know Grandma's sick!" He wanted to reach out and touch Pete, but his brother turned away and walked slowly down the yard.

Mark sank down on the steps again, watching him. "Who will take care of you?" Mark thought again. "Who will take care of *me*?" It was scary. There was Aunt Agnes, but she had weird ideas about what was good for Pete. She loved them. He knew that, but she and Grandma never agreed on what should be done about Pete.

Mark would always remember what he called the "day of the hurricane," even though it had been bright and sunny. It was the day Aunt Agnes had finally persuaded Grandma that Peter should be in a school. On the first day, Pete went to a "special" class that was held in the same school that Mark went to. They had been there only about an hour when Pete's teacher sent for Mark to come and calm down his brother. When Mark arrived, Pete was sitting at a little desk, his small shoulders shaking with sobs. He threw his arms around Mark and wouldn't let go. "Wanna' go home! Wanna' go home!" he shouted. It had taken a long time to find out what had happened, but it seemed that Pete had been hugging everybody and shouting. Even though he was only trying to be friendly, he had scared some of the kids. Half of them were crying, and the other half were pointing their fingers at Pete and laughing. Grandma had come to school to get him, and she never let him go back after that. Even though Aunt Agnes pleaded and explained that it was just one bad experience and that schools had changed since then, Pete had never gone back to school.

"I'll take care of Peter," Grandma insisted. "Nobody *here* will laugh at him. And that's final." It was, too. Aunt Agnes couldn't get another word out of Grandma on that subject, at least until her next visit.

Remembering, Mark sighed and shook his head. He watched Pete, who was now sitting in the dirt and playing. At least he was quiet. In fact, everything was quiet. The only sound was the hum of a tractor off in a field someplace. There was no loud, whistling breathing. That must mean that Grandma was better! The medicine Dr. Ramirez had brought must have helped her.

Not daring to move, he strained his ears to listen and heard a sound behind him on the step. He turned and saw Dr. Ramirez standing there looking down at him. The doctor's eyes were squinted against the sun, but they were unnaturally bright and shiny, as though he were about to cry.

Mark felt his heart begin to pound wildly. "Grandma?" he asked. "How's Grandma?"

For a long minute, Dr. Ramirez didn't answer. He didn't even seem to hear. He sat down on the step beside Mark. Slowly, almost carefully, he placed his elbows on his knees and then lowered his face into his hands. "Mark?" he said quietly, his voice muffled.

Something inside of Mark froze. It stopped moving and felt stiff, a hard little knot right in his center. He would just hold still and nothing would happen. Everything would be all right, just as it had been before Dr. Ramirez came out of the house.

"Don't let him speak," Mark prayed. "Don't let him say anything."

"Mark." Dr. Ramirez said. "Mark, your grandma's dead. I did everything I could to help her. *Everything*."

Mark didn't answer. Nothing was happening. He felt nothing. No pain. No tears. Dead. He shook his head. "No," he said.

Dr. Ramirez shook his head, too, his face still buried in his hands, so that he seemed to rock himself from side to side. "I'm sorry," he said softly.

Still Mark felt nothing.

The doctor touched Mark's hand for a second, then moved his own hand away. He didn't say anything else for a long time. When he finally did speak, he lifted his head, but his voice was strange, as though he were far away. He looked at Mark, his eyes shiny again. "You know," he said, "she tried not to die. I've never seen anyone try so hard."

Mark swallowed, and tears sprang to his eyes. Words, unbidden, leaped into his head, Grandma's words. "Your mom and daddy, they didn't want to leave you." Somewhere deep within something began to move. That frozen thing was moving inside, coming up from his stomach to his throat to choke him.

"No!" he cried out. Dr. Ramirez put his arms around him, and both of them began to cry.

"Looka'! Looka'!" It was Pete, screaming and squealing with delight. "Looka', I caught! Looka', I caught!" He had a big white duck in his arms, squeezing it hard against his middle.

The duck was flapping, turning its head this way and that, trying to nip at Pete's arms. "Looka', Mark!" Pete shouted. "A duck, I caught a duck!"

For a moment, Mark didn't answer. "A duck. Dead duck. Grandma's dead. A dead duck." He almost laughed.

"See, Mark?" Pete was still calling.

Mark rubbed his eyes with his fist. "Pete," he called. He had to tell him, had to tell him right now, or he wouldn't be able to tell him at all. "Pete?" he called again. "Come here."

Pete tried to stand up, but he was still holding the duck. He wobbled and almost fell over.

"Pete, come on," Mark called again. His voice sounded odd, as if it weren't even his own.

"Coming! Hold your shirt on!" Pete laughed the way he always did when he repeated something he had heard Mark say. He looked around once more, as though he didn't know what to do with the duck. Finally, reluctantly, he let it go. The duck flapped wildly, skimmed over the water, and then splashed into the pond, out beyond reach. Slowly, Pete came up to the porch.

"Pete?" Mark said, when his brother got there. "Sit down."

Pete plopped down.

"Pete?" Mark stopped, swallowed, then tried again. "Pete, you know Grandma's been sick? Right? Well, she died. She's dead, Pete."

Without knowing it was going to happen, Mark began crying, but Pete looked as though he hadn't heard anything. Mark closed his eyes and bit his lip, fighting back the thing that threatened to choke him.

There was a small tap-tapping on his knee, and he opened his eyes. Pete was looking at him somberly, patting his knee with two fingers. He smiled hopefully when Mark opened his eyes.

"Pete, do you understand? Grandma's dead."

Pete nodded, then repeated the word. "Dead!" He smiled at Mark, then said it again, as if he were practicing a new word. "Dead! Dead!" He was shouting and laughing.

"Shush!" Mark said. "Do you understand what I said, Pete?"

Pete nodded vigorously, his head going way up and then way down. But he was still smiling.

Dr. Ramirez put a hand on Mark's knee and whispered something to him.

Mark nodded and turned back to Pete. *"Gone,"* Mark said. "Pete, Grandma's gone, for good. Dead." He looked closely into Pete's face again, at Pete's big brown eyes just staring back at him. Pete looked so blank, so—*dumb*!

But suddenly Pete nodded, as though he had just figured something out. He stood, smiled, and started slowly back to the duck pond. As he went, he was whispering softly to himself, practicing his new word. "Dead. Grandma's dead."

IV

When Pete left, Dr. Ramirez stood up slowly. "Mark," he said, "I'm going in to make some phone calls. I think your Aunt Agnes should be called first."

Mark nodded, but he didn't speak. Aunt Agnes. What would *she* do? Come here and take over? Take Grandma's place? In his mind, he heard again the dozens of whispered conversations between Grandma and Aunt Agnes, Aunt Agnes urging Grandma to "do something" about Peter. Mark liked Aunt Agnes, loved her, even. She was good to him and Pete, gave them presents and everything, but he didn't want to see her now. What could she do, now that Grandma was ... dead?

Dr. Ramirez was still on the step. Mark looked up and was surprised at the uncertainty in the doctor's face. "Mark?" Dr. Ramirez said. "Would you like to come in and see Grandma?"

Mark shook his head hard. "No!"

Dr. Ramirez nodded as though he understood, and he went into the house.

For a long time after that Mark sat on the steps, sometimes just staring, sometimes crying quietly. It wasn't fair! Grandma shouldn't die. He was lonely for her, and now he and Pete were alone—all, all alone. What would become of them? He could hear Dr. Ramirez inside on the telephone, and his head just swam with thoughts and worries, some that didn't even make any sense. Once, Dr. Ramirez came out and asked Mark what he wanted for the funeral. What did he *want?* He didn't want a funeral. He wanted Grandma not to be dead. But Dr. Ramirez went on, telling him how Grandma would have wanted to have the wake at home, how the neighbors would come to visit, and how Mr. Mullins from the funeral home would come to prepare Grandma's body. Mark laughed when the doctor said that. *Prepare* Grandma's body? For what? For dying? She was dead, wasn't she? Besides, it didn't seem to matter to Mark now what they did. He even wondered how Dr. Ramirez could make all these plans. He and Grandma had been such good friends. At one time, Mark had even asked Grandma if she was going to marry him. But Grandma had only laughed and said, "Now, go on." But if they were such good friends, how could he be doing what he was doing?

It didn't matter to Mark. "You do it," was all he could say to the doctor. Dr. Ramirez had nodded and put a hand on Mark's shoulder, then gone back into the house and to the telephone.

Dr. Ramirez must have called half the neighborhood because by midafternoon at least a dozen cars had pulled up in front of the house. Neighbors came with food and flowers, and then the shiny black car came that said "CYRIL T. MULLINS FUNERAL HOME" on the side. Mark was still sitting on the steps when a taxi pulled up and Aunt Agnes got out. A taxi! Aunt Agnes had never taken a taxi to their house that Mark could remember. She always walked the mile from her house to theirs, but today she was carrying things—two shopping bags and a big suitcase. She was moving in!

Mark stood up as she came up the walk. Aunt Agnes wasn't nearly as old as Grandma, but she had pure white hair. She was small and round and waddled as she walked. When she saw Mark, she set down her bags and reached out to him. He went to her, and she put her arms around him and rocked him gently back and forth. But because she was smaller than Mark, it was as though Mark were rocking her. For a moment, it reminded him of when he was little and Grandma used to rock him like that. Then he was fighting back tears again.

He pulled away, bent down, and picked up her bags. "I'll take these for you," he said.

"Thank you, Mark." Aunt Agnes put a hand on his shoulder as they went up the walk. "How's Peter?"

"Okay, I guess."

"Does he understand?"

Mark shook his head. "I told him, but I don't know. You know Pete."

Aunt Agnes only sighed.

They went into the house together, but Mark put the bags down just inside the door and went out again. He wasn't going to take them into Grandma's room. And where else could he put them? Besides, there were too many people there, and he didn't want to talk to them right now. He went out to find Pete.

The next few days went by in a blur. There were only a few things that stood out clearly, that he would remember forever. There was the shiny gray casket that stood in one corner of the living room, surrounded by candles and flowers, but that he couldn't bring himself to look into. Pete didn't go in the living room either, seeming to know there was something too sad there to face. The other thing he would remember was the funeral, listening to Reverend Walker talk about Grandma and how good she had been and how she could see them from her place in heaven. Mark would always remember that because he knew it was a big lie, and ministers shouldn't lie. He wished it were true, but it wasn't. If Grandma could see him, she'd talk to him, wouldn't she? And he knew she wasn't doing that.

But the most scary thing about those days was the worry, trying to figure out what the grownups were doing, what they were planning. What would Aunt Agnes do about Pete? For days there had been hushed conversations inside the house.

Aunt Agnes had taken Mark aside that first night, quietly reassuring him that she was going to care for him and Pete now, that she had already put in for her retirement from teaching. But she was saying other things privately to Dr. Ramirez and some other grownups, and it was bad because they all stopped talking the minute Mark or Pete walked into the room.

On the night of the funeral, the two boys lay on their beds in their room next to the kitchen. Pete fell asleep right away, but Mark stayed awake, listening to the voices of Dr. Ramirez and Aunt Agnes drone on in the next room. The voices raised and dropped, and he caught only snatches of what was said, but some words came clearly.

"Of course I'll care for them." It was Aunt Agnes. "Don't even have to . . ." The voice dropped away. "Mumble, mumble, always said . . . mumble, own flesh and blood. But Peter goes, mumble, special school, mumble. Just can't, mumble . . ."

Mark held his breath. His heart was beating hard in his throat. He knew it, knew this would happen! He had known it ever since Grandma first got sick.

The other voice answered then, but he couldn't hear what was said. He threw back the sheet and climbed out of bed. Silently he crept across the room and opened the bedroom door a crack. The light from the kitchen fell in a thin line across the bedroom floor. Mark squinted against the light. Dr. Ramirez and Aunt Agnes were at the kitchen table drinking coffee, but there was no tablecloth on it. Grandma would be furious! She'd be so mad if she saw them doing that. She *always* put a cloth on, even if they were just having a snack.

"I know," Dr. Ramirez was saying. "I think you're right. In spite of what Mary felt, we have to think now what's best for Pete and what's best for you, Agnes. You can't cope with that situation all day."

They both nodded, but neither spoke again for a long time.

From his place by the door, Mark could feel his face get hot. They were sneaks! Dirty sneaks! Planning behind his back, planning behind Grandma's back! What did they know about Pete and what was good for him? They didn't care. All they cared about was themselves. The words pounded in his ears, as though they had been shouted instead of whispered. "You can't cope with that situation all day. Special school." Away! Away! They would send Pete away! He would really be all alone.

"What about Mark?" Dr. Ramirez spoke.

Mark held his breath.

"What about him?" Aunt Agnes asked.

"Well, we know how he feels about Pete and schools. Separating them would be awfully hard on Mark just now." The doctor paused. "Mark was 100 percent with Mary on that. Even though he hardly ever said anything about it, you could tell. And although I support this decision, we have to do some work before we break the news to him. We have to find out what you can afford. Maybe the state institution is the best answer because there isn't that much money and Mark is entitled to his education, too. But anyway, let's give some thought to it before we bring up the subject. It's very hard on Mark. Very hard."

Aunt Agnes nodded. "I know," she said softly. "Such a hard time for him, losing his family all over again."

"It might be a good idea to just ease him into the talk of school," Dr. Ramirez suggested.

"It's a good idea to do it soon," Aunt Agnes agreed. "With summer vacation here, we have a few weeks before school starts. We can start suggesting it, hinting—"

Mark didn't wait to hear any more about how they were going to break the news to him. He tiptoed back to his bed and lay down quietly. He made a decision, one that had really been in the back of his mind for a long time—ever since Grandma got so sick.

He waited for Dr. Ramirez to go home, for the house to be quiet, and for Aunt Agnes to go to bed. He felt mixed up, sad, and angry. He didn't feel mad at Aunt Agnes. It wasn't her fault. She was old, and he could see that she didn't really know how to take care of Pete, anyway.

He heard Dr. Ramirez say good night. The doctor's car started up, coughed and died, and started again. Mark listened while Aunt Agnes locked the front door, turned out the lights, then looked in on him and Pete. She stopped at his bed, then moved over to Pete's bed, bent down, and fixed the covers. Softly, she shut their door, and he could hear her go down the hall to her room—the room Grandma used to sleep in.

When the house was quiet, Mark got out of bed. He took the big canvas knapsack that had once been his father's and began stuffing it with the things they would need. Then he made a silent trip to the kitchen.

When the bag was filled, Mark dressed himself and got out Pete's things. He tiptoed to his brother's bed. Pete was lying on his stomach, breathing deeply, his arms hanging over the side of the bed. Mark touched his back. "Pete? Pete? Wake up!"

Pete sat up. Before he could say a word, Mark said, "Shush! Don't say anything, Pete. Now, listen! I have a surprise for you. Want to go someplace with me? Just you and me?"

Pete nodded. He smiled sleepily.

"Get up, then," Mark whispered. "But remember, don't say a word. *Just be quiet.* We're going someplace special. Just you and me!"

V

A square of moonlight lay across the bed as Mark helped Pete do the things his brother had trouble with, such as his shoelaces, and then they were ready. Silently, they tiptoed from their room and across the kitchen and unlocked the door. "Pete, don't trip!" Mark prayed. But Pete was tiptoeing beside him, as quiet as Mark himself was.

Outside, the moon bathed the yard with light as they made their way toward the gate. Mark looked back once at the house, and his eyes filled with tears as he remembered the nights that he and Grandma had sat on the porch swing, talking about school or about something funny that Pete had done that day.

Suddenly Pete began to shout. "Hey! Hey! Duck!" He was running across the yard and heading for the duck pond! The ducks were curled up in the sand near the pond, their heads under their wings.

Mark raced after him. "Pete! Peter! Shush up!" he whispered frantically. If Pete woke the ducks, there would be such squawking and noise that Aunt Agnes would be out here in a second!

But Pete was too fast for him and had already reached the pond. For a second he seemed to hesitate as he looked over the ducks. Then he pounced on one, snatched it up, and in an instant was through the gate and running down the road, the duck flapping and squawking under his arm.

The other ducks were stirring too as Mark fled after Pete. When they were out of sight of the house, they stopped.

Mark leaned against a tree, breathing hard. "You're a pain, you know that?" he said angrily. "A real pain! Now what'd you do that for?"

Pete shrugged.

"I mean it," Mark said. "Why'd you do that?"

Pete stuck out his lower lip, then turned his back. "It's *my* duck."

"Well, that's dumb!" Mark said. "You almost woke up Aunt Agnes. Besides, we can't go where we're going carrying a duck."

Pete didn't turn around. "It's my duck!" He shouted again over his shoulder.

"Shush!" Mark hissed at him. He glared at Pete's back. His brother looked really stupid, holding the huge duck. Its feet were hanging down, and it flapped and squirmed to be free. Dumb duck. Mark sighed. Well, at least the duck wasn't squawking anymore. He knew it was stupid to take the duck with them, but he also knew it was useless to argue with Pete once his brother had made up his mind. "All right," he said grudgingly. "You win. Now turn around."

But Pete didn't budge.

"Come on, turn around. You can take your duck."

Slowly, Pete turned around.

Mark glared at him for a minute, then began to smile in spite of himself. "Pete," he said. "Tell me something. How'd you know which one was your duck? I mean, how'd you pick her out in the dark from all the other ducks?"

Pete frowned. "This duck?"

"Yeah, that duck. How'd you know it was yours?"

" 'Cause!" Pete answered. He looked down at the duck in his arms, and then up at Mark again. " 'Cause it's . . . my . . . duck," he said slowly and carefully, as though explaining something to a child. "Know that?"

"Yeah, but . . . Never mind," Mark said. He picked up the heavy knapsack and lifted it to his shoulder.

"Where we going? You and me?" Pete asked.

"To the lake," Mark said. "Now shush!" he added quickly. He could feel Pete warming up to shout again now that he knew where they were going. Pete loved the lake and staying in the cabin there. Every year—before this one, when Grandma got so sick—they spent most of the summer there. It was Pete's favorite place. Grandma had told Mark once that he and Pete really owned the cabin because it had belonged to their parents. "Now listen," Mark continued quietly. "It's a very long walk, but we can do it. Right?"

Pete nodded.

"Okay. We're going to stay in the cabin. Just you and me. Okay?" Mark patted his pocket. "I have the key right here."

"Okay!" Pete shouted.

"Pe-ter!" Mark said, exasperated. They'd never

make it to the lake without being found if Pete didn't stop shouting. He had an idea. Carefully, he reached over and put one finger on Pete's lips just as Grandma had done. "Hush," he whispered. "Hush? Okay?"

Pete smiled. "Okay." He said it more quietly than before but still awfully loud. "How come?"

"Because. Grandma said."

Pete smiled. "Grandma said," he whispered.

The sun was overhead by the time Mark and Pete turned into the path that led to the cabin and the lake. Mark knew they had walked about twenty miles, but from the way his feet were burning, it felt more like a hundred. The tar had become soft, swelling up in little blisters from the heat. They had walked along the edge of the road, partly to stay off the hot tar, but also to be ready to dive into the tall grasses if a car went by. Mark didn't want anyone to see them walking toward the lake. They had to hide in the grass only once, and that was early in the morning before the sun was up.

As they turned into the deep, rutted path that led to the lake, Mark turned his head to look around, taking in his surroundings almost hungrily. The path was the same as it had been for as long as he could remember—ruts on each side where cars had made tracks for years of summers. Chipmunks scurried across the road, their tails pointed up as they dived for cover into their holes. Overhead were the old, familiar trees, so thick that Mark could barely see the sky until a breeze blew and shifted the leaves, revealing patches of blue.

As they got closer to the lake, Mark felt himself breathing easier, as if some of the knots and hurting places that had been inside him ever since Grandma first got so sick were beginning to let go. He took a deep breath that was almost a sigh and looked at Pete. Pete felt good, too. Mark could tell. Quietly, not making a sound, he was shuffling through the moldy leaves. Even the duck in his arms was quiet and sleepy-looking. Mark hoped the duck wasn't as thirsty as he was.

Suddenly, the silence was broken by a whining, angry sound like the drone of a mosquito. Motorboats! Of course. How could he have forgotten? There would be other vacationers on the lake. But the vacation cottages were spread pretty far apart. If they could just avoid being seen, he was sure that he and Pete could stay here for a few days—at least until he could think of someplace else to go. Aunt Agnes and Dr. Ramirez wouldn't think of looking here, not right away, anyway. They would never believe that he and Pete would walk that far.

He had been so busy thinking that he hadn't noticed Pete stop in front of him, and he almost walked up his brother's back. Pete was standing at the edge of the path, staring off in the direction of a cabin in the woods. He turned to Mark, wide-eyed, then turned back, pointing.

Mark's eyes followed Pete's pointing finger. There, in a little clearing behind a small gray cabin, three deer grazed. Someone, a man, was in the clearing, about an arm's length away from the deer. He was standing perfectly still, holding a bucket in his outstretched hand.

One of the deer, a doe, approached the man. Slowly she bent her head and began nibbling from the bucket. A second deer, a small fawn, came closer. It, too, began eating from the bucket.

Mark and Pete watched in wonder.

The third deer stood motionless. She looked toward Mark and Pete. Her ears were pointed high, and she shifted restlessly once and took a sideward step. Then she must have given a signal, for suddenly all three deer took off into the forest. Silently they leaped the small rail fence, flicked their white tails, and were gone.

It was the signal for Pete to move. With the duck tucked under one arm, he began crashing through the underbrush, clearing the way with his free hand. "Mister! Hey, Mister?" he shouted.

"Pete! Pe-ter!" Mark called frantically to his brother. "Pete, come here!" But Pete kept going. Mark followed, trying to catch up with him, but Pete didn't stop until he stood in the clearing next to the man.

The man wasn't very tall—hardly bigger than Mark—but he was square and strong-looking. His face was tanned and lined, and he was squinting so that Mark could barely see his eyes. But when he spoke, his voice was soft. "So!" he said. He smiled, and his eyes reappeared, a bright blue. "So you're the reason why my friends took off in such a hurry."

"We didn't mean to scare them," Mark said, before Pete could say anything. He was close enough then to grab Pete's shirt. "Come on, Pete," he whispered, and he tugged at him.

"No!" Pete shouted.

"Come on!" Mark said through his teeth, trying to convey a signal to his brother, but Pete didn't notice. He stood there as if he were planted, his arms wrapped tightly around the duck, which was agitated now, flapping and snapping its head back and forth. Its feathers were all squashed and matted where Pete had been holding it. "See the deer!" Pete shouted, holding the duck firmly.

Mark looked from Pete back to the man, who was frowning at them now. Suddenly, in his mind, Mark had a picture of how he and Pete must look: Pete with the stupid duck, he with the knapsack. He began trying to make up a story to explain what they were doing there. But before he could speak, the man said, "You summer people?"

Mark nodded.

"I didn't know there were summer people this part of the lake," the man said. He didn't sound happy about it, but he held out his hand. "My name's Eric."

Pete held the duck tightly in one arm and grabbed Eric's outstretched hand with his free one. "I'm Pete!" he shouted. "He's Mark!" He was standing close to Eric, still holding his hand, but he was really shouting. "Are the deer coming back?"

Eric looked surprised. "Not if you keep making so much noise!" But then he added more softly, "Yes, they'll be back. Tonight. And tomorrow around sunrise." He smiled at Pete then, looking at the duck in his arms. "Is that your pet?"

"It's my *duck*!" Pete answered.

"Come on, Pete." Mark nudged him. "Come on, let's go."

"No, gonna' wait!"

"You can't!" Mark said. He was beginning to feel desperate. He could feel Eric's eyes on them, and he even imagined he knew what Eric was thinking: "Something's wrong. These kids shouldn't be here." How could Mark get Pete away? Pete had already said too much—told their names when nobody was even supposed to know where they were. "Come on, Pete, please?" Mark said almost pleadingly. "Look, we can come back tomorrow morning before the sun is even up, okay? I promise. But you've got to come now."

"No!" Pete shouted.

Mark took a deep breath. "Come on, Pete, please? Tomorrow, I promise."

"Why don't you come in the morning?" Eric said. He was looking at Pete with a funny expression on his face. "The deer will be back then." He said it simply and quietly, as though he were speaking to a very small child.

Pete bent his head and buried his face in the duck's feathers. For a long moment he stayed that way and then looked up and sighed. "Okay," he said sadly.

Mark smiled with relief. "Thanks, Pete!"

"You come back in the morning then," Eric said. "But remember, come like the deer, very quietly." He put one finger on his lips, and he smiled.

Pete smiled, too, putting one finger on his lips. "Grandma said," he said to Eric.

VI

Mark and Pete continued to the foot of the dirt path. There, in a little clearing at the end of the road, stood the gray, weathered cabin, its windows and porches still covered with the boards put up last fall. Here the lake began, and the woods stretched out behind them. For a moment, Mark felt sad, remembering how he and Grandma used to argue about whether everything—the woods, the lake, the road—all ended or began here. It wasn't really arguing, only fooling. Mark always said everything ended here, but Grandma only laughed and said you couldn't be sure.

Putting down the heavy knapsack, Mark turned to Pete, but Pete was gone. "Pete! Peter!" he called. There was a splash and a shout from behind the cabin, and in a moment Pete reappeared. He was dripping wet, his shirt clinging to his body. For the first time since early that morning, he didn't have the duck in his arms.

"Did you put her in the lake?" Mark asked.

"She *bit* me!" Pete shouted. He didn't look injured, but he had that sulky look he got when his feelings were hurt.

"Smart duck!" Mark said, but he laughed. "She didn't mean it." He put a hand on Pete's arm. "Come on. We have work to do."

Together, they began getting the cabin ready to be lived in again. Mark was surprised at how well they worked together. They had done this so many times with Grandma that they knew just what to do. With a heavy, iron spike, kept under the porch for that purpose, they pried loose the boards that covered the screens, porches, and windows, and then stacked the boards under the porch. Mark made sure that each was put away in order, so they could put them back in place when they were ready to leave. He hadn't figured out where they'd go yet, but he knew he'd think of someplace.

When they finished outdoors, Mark unlocked the door and they went in, Pete following so close on Mark's heels that he almost tripped them both. The cabin smelled as if it had been buried in pine needles and wet leaves all winter, but it was a good smell, and Mark breathed deeply.

"Stinks!" Pete shouted, and he pinched his nose.

Mark laughed. It did smell funny, but not bad, just moist and musty. He put the key on its nail in the kitchen, then opened the other door, which faced the side. A breeze swept through, bringing new odors, of the lake and of summer, and with them a flood of memories.

Mark looked around the cabin. It wasn't very big.

One large area served as the kitchen, living room, and dining room, all in one; and there were two small bedrooms. The walls between them were thin partitions that went partway up to the ceiling. It was always easy to hear what was going on in the other rooms, and now, as Mark began cleaning up the kitchen, he could hear Pete on the other side of the wall, opening and shutting dresser drawers, discovering the place all over again. He hummed as he banged, and he sounded happy, as though he had just been set free.

It was almost dark by the time the cabin was cleaned and aired. Mark had already turned on the electricity by flicking the switch in the bathroom next to the hot-water heater, but he decided not to turn on a lamp yet. There was still enough light to see by, and he wanted to enjoy this time of night. It was the time he liked best, when it was almost, but not quite, dark.

He went out onto the porch that faced the lake and sat on the steps, thinking, feeling contented, happy almost. How good it was to be here! If only Grandma were here, too. He watched Pete, who was sitting on the dock that jutted out into the water, sitting perfectly still, staring into the lake. He knew Pete was playing his favorite game. For as long as Mark could remember, little sunfish had made their home at the foot of the dock. In the clear water, you could see them swishing back and forth over their sandy nest. Every summer night for years, Pete had tried to catch a fish in his bare hands. He had never caught one, but he had never stopped trying either. Mark and Grandma used to bet on whether or not he ever would.

Now, as Mark watched, he wondered what Pete

thought about the fish. "Hey, Pete?" he called softly.

Pete didn't answer.

"Hey, Pete? What are you doing?"

"Nothing." The answer came softly. No shouting this time.

"Come on, you're looking at something. What?" Mark realized suddenly that he really didn't know what went on in Pete's head when he saw deer or ducks or fish, and he wanted to know.

But still Pete didn't answer. Quietly and slowly, he put one hand up as though silencing Mark. Then, with a sudden tumbling motion, he fell or dived head-first into the lake. Water splashed everywhere, and the dock was suddenly soaked as Pete kicked and flailed. For a moment he was gone.

Mark stood up, waiting for Pete to come back up. He was a good swimmer, but still Mark was relieved when he reappeared. He was dripping everywhere, his hair plastered close to his head. He looked sad and held out both hands—empty. "Fish gone!" he shouted.

Mark laughed. "Come on, Pete, forget them. Come on up and let's have supper. It's almost dark." Mark wasn't hungry because they had eaten some sandwiches before, but he was suddenly lonely here in the gathering darkness, and he wanted Pete's company.

Slowly Pete came out of the water, shaking himself hard, as a dog would do, water droplets spinning from him.

"Come on," Mark urged him.

"Keep your shirt on," Pete called back, but he laughed and slowly lumbered up to the porch.

Mark went to the kitchen, made sandwiches, then

brought them to the porch and gave one to his brother. Pete ate slowly, intently, the way he always did, as though eating were a big problem that he had to figure out. He said nothing until he had finished, but then he stood up and looked at Mark. "Deer!" he announced.

"What?"

"See the deer!" Pete said loudly.

"Hey, Pete, shush up, will you?" Mark looked around. "Just shush. We'll be in big trouble if anybody knows we're here. Now listen, I told you before, we can't see the deer tonight. But remember? I promised we'd go tomorrow."

Pete got a sullen look again and folded his arms.

Quickly, trying to head off another argument, Mark said, "Pete, I have an idea. How about if we go swimming? Maybe you could even catch your fish."

"Okay!" Pete shouted.

Mark shook his head. Sometimes he got really tired of Pete. Here it was, the first day he was taking care of Pete by himself, and he was sick of him already. Pain, pain, pain! How could Grandma have put up with him all day long? Nevertheless, he leaned over and put one finger gently on Pete's lips as he had done that morning. "Will you hush?"

Pete just nodded.

"Okay, let's go," Mark said. "But we can't go out far. It's almost dark."

Together, they went down the steps to the dock, stripped off their clothes, and stepped into the water.

Mark went in slowly, gasping as the water came up around his middle. He had forgotten how cold this lake was! But Pete didn't seem to care. He dived headfirst, kicking and splashing, stirring up mud from the bottom.

After Mark got used to the water, he began to enjoy swimming again. Even though the lake was deep and very cold, he had never been afraid of it. He was a good, strong swimmer. Pete, too. Grandma had made sure of that. He lay on his back now, looking up at the darkening sky. Suddenly, a bright streak appeared, shooting downward across the sky, as though it were heading for the lake. A shooting star! Mark tried to point it out to Pete, but by the time his brother looked up, the star was gone.

Mark smiled. A shooting star! A sign of good luck. This was the right place to be! And tomorrow he would go with Pete to see the deer again.

VII

The sun was already high when Mark woke next morning. He blinked and shook his head. He had slept so soundly. He sat up, rubbed his eyes, and glanced at his watch. Eight o'clock!

He flopped back on the bed and looked around the room. How pretty it was in here, the sun streaming across the bare floorboards. He stretched, then lay there for a moment, thinking. He figured he and Pete could probably stay a few more days before anyone would think of looking for them here. After that— Well, after a few days, maybe they'd go to a city. He had always wanted to go to a city, and in the crowds, no one would find them. Probably he could get a job there, maybe working in a store, and that way he could pay for the food and things he and Pete would need. If he could just find a place with a playground for Pete, maybe with swings, then Pete would be happy until Mark came back for him each day.

Mark glanced over at the next bed, but Pete was already gone, probably down at the dock trying to catch the fish again. Mark smiled, remembering how forlorn Pete had looked last night when he didn't catch anything. He'd better get up now and check on Pete.

Slowly, he got out of bed and went to the front porch, which overlooked the lake and the dock. No Pete there. Could he be playing with the duck somewhere?

Mark went back to the bedroom to dress, then went to the kitchen to plan breakfast. He had brought with him peanut butter and bread and cookies. That with some powdered stuff to drink should make a pretty good breakfast. But he needed to get Pete first.

He went back to the screened-in porch. "Pete!" he called. "Hey, Pete! Where are you? Breakfast time."

He didn't see his brother anywhere, and even if Pete had answered, he probably wouldn't have heard him. It was suddenly so noisy out on the lake. A motorboat was roaring and turning and making waves, pulling a water skier along in its wake. Mark wished they'd go away. How could Pete hear him calling over that racket?

He waited before calling again, knowing the skier would fall off soon. It always happened that way, and then the boat would slow its motor and come back. He didn't have to wait long. In a minute, he saw his prediction come true, and in the sudden silence, Mark called, "Pete? Hey, Peter! Breakfast."

He waited. Still no answer. The man on the boat heard, though, and he looked over at Mark, raising one hand in a silent wave. Mark waved back. It was dangerous to call like this. Somebody might come over to talk, and then . . .

Opening the screen door on the front porch, Mark went down the steps and along the path to the dock. He waited until the boat had picked up the skier and was off again. "Pete?" he called softly. "Pete?"

Silence.

Darn! Was Pete hiding? He did that sometimes, then jumped out, trying to scare Mark. Half the time it worked, too. He scared Mark practically to death. Mark went back to the house then and circled it slowly, looking carefully under the porches in case Pete jumped out at him. "Pete! Hey, Pete?" he called. "Are you hiding? Come on, cut it out! It's time for breakfast."

There was still no answer.

Why was Pete such a nuisance? Couldn't he act like a normal kid just once? Mark ran up the steps. Maybe Pete had come in while he was looking outside. He opened the door and called into the house. "Pete? Pete!"

Only silence.

Suddenly a tightness formed in Mark's throat, and his heart began beating wildly. Pete was lost, just as he had been that day last summer! Only this time there was no one around to help look for him. "Cut it out!" he told himself. "Don't be dumb! Pete's around here somewhere. You just have to find out where."

He ran down the steps again. Quickly this time, he circled the house. "Pete! Peter?" Running hard, he went farther back into the woods, back to the shed in which they kept the rakes and equipment, back to the trash and mulch piles. Not there. Then, still running, he went back to the lake. He forced himself to go out to the end of the dock and to look into the water. It was deep out there. Pete was a good swimmer, but . . . Mark took a deep breath. There was no Pete!

Then, making himself slow down and act normally, he returned to the cabin and went around it once more. Then he remembered. Pete fell asleep lots of times just anywhere at all, wherever he got tired! Grandma found him once sleeping in the bathtub, and another time right in the middle of the yard.

Mark ran into the house. To the bathroom. To the back porch. To Grandma's room. No Pete.

The choking feeling got worse. "Oh, no!" he prayed. "Please, God, please no."

Tears came to his eyes, but he wouldn't cry. He couldn't. He had to find Pete. But where? "Where are you?" he wanted to scream. Instead he laughed out loud. Boy, was he dumb! Pete was smart compared to him. The deer! He was supposed to go out with Pete early to see the deer. Pete hadn't waited for him to wake up. He had gone by himself.

Quickly, running hard, Mark started out for Eric's house. He was out of breath by the time he got there. He looked around the yard, but there was no sign of Pete—at least not yet. But he could be anywhere, even inside the cabin. He did that often, walked right into people's houses, sometimes even without being invited.

Mark waited a moment by the fence until he had caught his breath. His heart was still pounding like crazy, but it wasn't just from running. He was scared and would be until he had found his brother.

Then everything would be all right. But he knew now he'd have to watch Pete more closely. If Grandma knew that Pete had disappeared, even for a minute . . .

Quietly, Mark went around the house and looked into the front yard, afraid to call out since Eric might hear him. But Pete wasn't there. Then he *had* to be in the house. Mark hated to knock, not wanting to answer any questions Eric might ask, but he knew he'd have to. Knowing Pete, Mark realized his brother had probably told Eric everything by now, anyway.

Tiptoeing, Mark went up the steps to the cabin door, thinking perhaps he would hear voices, but no sound came from inside. He raised his hand and knocked.

Almost immediately, Eric opened the door. He was wearing the same plaid shirt he had worn yesterday, but now he was also wearing glasses. He took the glasses off and smiled. "Hello!" he said, and he sounded pleased to see Mark.

Mark tried to peer around him into the room. No Pete that he could see. "Hello," he said. But he couldn't bring himself to ask whether Peter was there.

Eric nodded, as if he knew what Mark wanted. "I know what you're looking for," he said. He smiled. "I'm afraid you're too late for that. Anyway, they never did come this morning."

"Who?"

"The deer. Isn't that what you . . . ?"

"Is my brother here?" Mark blurted it out.

"Your *brother*?"

"Yes, Pete! Is he here?"

Eric shook his head. "No, he's not."

"You mean you haven't seen him? Not at all? He didn't come here this morning?"

Eric shook his head again. He frowned in that way he had in which his eyes almost disappeared. "Your brother's not missing, is he?"

"Yes. I mean, no! Not missing. Just . . ." He felt sick and turned away.

Eric came out onto the porch and let the screen door slam shut behind him. He grasped Mark's shoulder lightly but forcefully enough to hold him back. "Don't go away," he said. "Tell me what's going on. Is Pete missing? Did something happen?"

"No." Mark shook his head and stepped away from Eric. "I have to go." He turned and ran down the steps.

When Mark was almost out of the yard, Eric called, "What about your parents? Do they know?"

Mark didn't bother to answer. "*Parents?*" He just shook his head and turned onto the path. He began running as fast as he could back toward the lake.

VIII

As Mark ran, he could feel the terror building inside him, pounding with his footsteps. He kept repeating to himself, "Nothing has happened to Pete. Nothing has happened. Nothing."

When he got closer to the cabin, he deliberately slowed to a walk. He would give Pete time to get back there first. Taking deep breaths to calm himself, he went up the porch steps. Slowly, trying to pretend it was any ordinary summer day, he opened the cabin door. "Pete?" he called. "Pe-ete!" He went into the house then and into each room. The sun still lay across the bedroom floor. The house was perfectly still.

"Nothing has happened to Pete!" Fighting the panic, he went through the house and out the back way, then down the steps to the dock. The dock and the lake were just as he had left them, tiny waves licking the edge of the pier.

Now he could feel his breath coming in big, shaky sobs. He went back to the porch and sat down, putting his head on his knees.

Was there a sound on the path? A car? He sat up, listening intently, his heart racing. But there was nothing. It must have been on the other side of the lake. He leaned back against the step, but he heard it again, clearly this time. It wasn't a car. There were footsteps inside the house! Scrambling to his feet, he ran up the steps and threw the screen door open. "Pete!" he shouted.

Someone was in the kitchen, but it wasn't Pete. It was someone big—a man.

It was hard to see, coming in from the sun like that. The man spoke. It was— Oh, no!

"Mark!" Dr. Ramirez said.

"What are you doing here?" Mark cried. He swallowed hard. *"Go away!"* he prayed silently. *"Go away!!"* How did the doctor get here? He must have come in the front way while Mark was around back. "What are you doing here?" Mark said again, out loud.

"Mark, we've been so worried!" the doctor said. "We've been practically out of our minds with worry and fear. Why did you run away? You shouldn't have done that."

"I didn't run away. I just left. Now you go too. Leave us alone!"

Dr. Ramirez came and stood beside him. "Mark, you can't do this. You and Pete can't live here all by yourselves. Even if you want to, you can't. You're only kids!"

"We can! Will you leave us alone?" Mark was frantic.

"Where's Pete?"

"Outside! With the fish."

Dr. Ramirez shook his head. "Come here." He sat down on the kitchen bench and patted a place alongside him. "Sit down and talk to me. What's going on?"

Mark took a step closer but didn't sit. With his eyes becoming accustomed to the semidarkness of the cabin, he could see the doctor's face more clearly. He was pale and tired-looking, and he suddenly seemed much older than he had ever seemed before. It was clear, too, that he hadn't shaved that day.

"Listen, Mark," Dr. Ramirez said. "I know you feel awful, like it's the end of the world. But trust me. It's going to be all right. It will get better. You'll miss your grandma terribly for a while. We all will. But believe me, you'll feel better. This running away won't solve anything."

Mark turned to the window and stared out, his heart pounding wildly. Oh, God, where was Pete! And Dr. Ramirez was here to preach to him. But he didn't dare move. He couldn't tell the doctor that Pete was lost.

"Mark?" Dr. Ramirez tried again. "I know you're angry, too. But this has happened to other people and they've survived. You're going to survive, too, you know. You're not all alone."

"You're right, I'm not!" Mark burst out. "I've got Pete. And Pete's got me." The words surprised him when they came out, his voice weird, tense, and choked-sounding. "We don't need anybody else."

"Well, perhaps." Dr. Ramirez seemed surprised. "But maybe somebody else needs *you*. Aunt Agnes cares about you a lot. She's been worried sick. I care about you. But you're right about having each other, and that's a lot." He paused and then added softly, "Just remember that others care."

"You big phony!" Suddenly Mark was crying. He didn't want to cry, yet tears were streaming down his cheeks. "You phony!" he cried again. "We don't have *anybody*. Not Grandma anymore. Not Aunt Agnes. Not you. Not anybody!" He kept his back turned, and he practically shouted the words over his shoulder. He tried to pitch his voice high, mimicking the words he had heard Aunt Agnes say that night. " 'Send Pete . . . special school somewhere!" He grabbed the windowsill so hard that his fingernails dug into the soft wood. "And *you*—you *agreed*. 'Send him to an institution. There's not enough money . . .' " He broke off. For two days those words had been buried in the back of his mind, but Mark knew now that they would be with him forever. Saying them out loud, he saw again the whole scene as clearly as though he were watching it through the crack in the bedroom door—Dr. Ramirez and Aunt Agnes planning to send Pete away, sitting at the table, on which there was no cloth.

For a moment, Mark felt nothing. He was numb, while silence surrounded him like cotton. Then he heard Dr. Ramirez move, and he felt the doctor's hand on his shoulder. He jerked away.

"I'm sorry you overheard that, Mark," Dr. Ramirez said. "I really am. We were only trying to think what's best for you."

"And not what's best for Pete!" He felt now as though his head would burst, as if his brain were on fire, but he plunged on. "You talk about Pete as though he were a—a *thing*! He's not a thing. He's a person! And he's *my* brother!" He gave up even trying for control.

He cried for a long time, with Dr. Ramirez beside him. The doctor had put his hand on Mark's shoulder again, and this time Mark didn't bother to pull away. After a few minutes, Dr. Ramirez spoke again. "I'm sorry. Maybe we made a mistake trying to decide your future without bringing you in on it. But decisions can be changed if necessary. Let's talk about it again, all of us together, Aunt Agnes, too. Okay?"

Mark didn't answer.

"Where's Pete?" Dr. Ramirez continued. "We really shouldn't leave him alone so long."

Mark looked up. "Pete's gone. He's lost." He was still crying, but he spoke calmly, his voice flat. Oddly, he felt better, relieved almost to finally say it out loud.

"What?" There was no understanding in the doctor's eyes.

"He's lost."

"What do you mean, he's lost?" Dr. Ramirez grasped Mark's shoulder hard, his eyes wide with fear. "Explain to me! Quickly." He was almost shaking Mark.

"I think he's looking for the deer." Mark struggled to find the right words. "See, I think that's where he went. But I looked for him. I went right back to that place, but he wasn't there. I ran all the way . . ."

"Wait a minute," Dr. Ramirez interrupted. Disbelief swept across his face. "Are you telling me that Peter is gone?"

Mark nodded.

"When did you see him last?"

"Last night, but . . ."

"Last night!" Dr. Ramirez dropped his hand from Mark's shoulder. "Go on," he said quietly.

Slowly, Mark told the doctor everything—about their seeing the deer, about Eric's house, and about Mark's promise to take Pete to see the deer this morning, but how, when he woke up, Pete was gone. And he hadn't been able to find his brother since.

When Mark was finished, Dr. Ramirez walked slowly across the room to the screen door and stood there, one fist clenched at his side, the other drumming gently against the door frame. Finally he turned around. "Okay, Mark," he said. "We have a lot of work to do, all of us. But the first thing to do is find Peter and to let Aunt Agnes know where you are. She's been worried to death about both of you."

"Don't tell her about Pete!"

"I have to. You know that. And I'm going to go get help, lots of it. We'll need to have people to search these woods. Now, I want you to stay here in case Pete comes back. I'll be back as soon as I can." He started out the door, then turned back. "Mark, don't worry. We'll find Pete. He can't have gone far. We'll get him out of these woods, and he'll be fine, as good as new."

Mark nodded, unable to speak. He wanted to believe, but he wasn't sure.

Dr. Ramirez nodded too, then turned and went out the door.

After a minute, Mark could hear the car start up, backing and turning in the narrow path. He sat down on the bench and pulled his knees up, wrapping his arms tightly around them. He put his head on his knees, sort of rocking himself. "Please, God, please," he prayed silently. Exactly what he was praying for, he didn't know, but he said over and over, "Please, God, please."

IX

It seemed an eternity to Mark as he sat alone in the cabin, watching the second hand on his watch creep around the dial. One minute, two minutes, three minutes. He wanted to run to Eric's house and look for Pete just once more—it was the only place Pete could possibly have gone—but Mark didn't dare leave. Pete might come back. Dr. Ramirez was probably right. Mark tried to picture what the doctor was doing now. He would drive to the nearest town on the other side of the lake. It would take maybe twenty minutes. And when he got there, whom would he call? The fire department? Probably, because they always sent out volunteers when there was trouble. And then, after he had called the fire department, he'd call Grandma. No, not Grandma! Her name had jumped into his head, and he felt as though he had to snatch it back. He spoke out loud, correcting what he had thought. "He'll call Aunt Agnes. He'll call *Aunt Agnes*."

He leaned against the wall, closing his eyes tightly. Aunt Agnes was going to be so upset! Now that they had been found, what would happen? Could he keep them from putting Pete in that— place? *If* they found Pete? *When* they found Pete! For a moment, Mark had a thought he'd had before, even when Grandma was alive. Maybe school wouldn't be that bad for Pete. At least that way there'd be someone to watch him, and no one would have to worry about his disappearing all the time. But then Mark felt almost ashamed of the thought. He could not send his brother away. He remembered how Grandma felt about it and how she always said, "No school. Just plain no!"

Twenty-five minutes, thirty, forty . . . He went out to the porch and looked at the lake. Noises on the path! He ran back into the house, through the kitchen, and looked out the door.

Dr. Ramirez's car was rumbling and bouncing across the stones. It stopped and the doctor got out, his eyebrows raised, his whole face asking the question he didn't ask out loud.

But Mark knew what he was asking. "No," he called. "Pete's not here."

Dr. Ramirez shook his head, his lips drawn together in a tight line. He walked into the house and went straight to the front porch, where he stood looking toward the lake. He didn't speak, and he seemed to be deep in thought.

Mark stood watching him, his whole body tense. He wanted to ask questions: "Did you call Aunt Agnes? What did she say?" But he didn't because he was afraid of the answers.

After a moment, Dr. Ramirez turned around. His face seemed even more lined than before, and his usually neat gray hair was rumpled. His unshaven chin was darker, too, giving his normally tanned face a pale, grayish look. He spoke quietly. "I called Aunt Agnes," he said, "and told her what had happened. I asked her to stay there. There's just a chance that Pete could find his way back. . . ."

"But it's so far! How could he find the way?"

"I don't know, but help is on the way. I talked to the fire department, and they sent out a call for volunteers. . . . Listen!"

They both went into the kitchen and looked out. A whole line of cars and jeeps were making their way into the woods. Some of the jeeps had spotlights on top. Within a few minutes, the kitchen was teeming with men. Some wore heavy hiking boots, and all carried lanterns or flashlights. Some even had walkie-talkies. They stood in the kitchen making plans, talking quietly among themselves, talking to Dr. Ramirez. Several of them looked curiously at Mark, but no one spoke to him.

Mark overheard words like deer hunters—poachers, they called them. A lot of the men had heard shots in the woods that morning. From the way they were talking, it sounded as though they thought Pete had been shot. Disgusted, Mark went out on the porch so he wouldn't hear any more. Pete hadn't been shot! He didn't know how he knew, but he knew. Pete had some problems, but he wasn't stupid! He wasn't dumb enough to go near someone with a gun! Pete was *lost*, not dead. Didn't they understand that? What they had to do was find him.

Restlessly, Mark paced from the porch to the kitchen, from the kitchen to the porch, then back again. Where was Pete? Finally, he sat down on the glider on the porch, letting his sneaker drag back and forth beneath him as he rocked. "Find Pete. Find Pete. Find Pete," the rocker squeaked.

It was late afternoon when something unusual appeared on the lake. Several large boats came close to shore, dragging ropes behind them that appeared to have a heavy object, an anchor or something, attached to them. What were they? Mark got off the swing, went into the kitchen where Dr. Ramirez was, and brought the doctor out to the porch with him. "What's that?" Mark asked, indicating the boats.

The doctor watched for a while, then turned to Mark. He looked at the boy silently as though debating something, but he didn't answer.

Mark turned away and looked through the screen again. Suddenly, he knew what the boats were doing! He remembered! They were dragging the lake, looking for Pete's body! He had seen it before, long ago when he was still little, when an old woman from the other side of the lake had disappeared and everybody thought she had fallen into the lake and drowned.

Dr. Ramirez put his hands on Mark's shoulders and turned him away from the lake to face the kitchen. "Don't worry!" he said softly, but there was something almost fierce in his voice. "Please don't worry. They're not going to find anything." He gave Mark a little push toward the kitchen. "Go get something to eat," he said. "Somebody brought sandwiches and fruit. What have you eaten today?"

Eaten? How could he eat? He didn't answer. Dr. Ramirez, who didn't appear to expect an answer anyway, turned back to watch the boats.

Mark watched, too, watched the boats trailing their iron hooks. Suddenly he jumped up. He was going to be sick, but he didn't run into the house. Instead, he ran down the steps and back into the woods and bent over a pile of old leaves. He hadn't eaten since yesterday, but still he vomited for a long time. He didn't know whether he was really sick or whether this was another kind of ache, similar to the one he had felt the day Grandma died. Only this was worse.

When he felt a little better, he stood up and took a deep breath. It was time to go. There was something he had to do.

Slowly, he went back into the cabin, washed up, then went to the kitchen. A fat man stood by the kitchen table. He wore a plaid shirt that stretched tightly over his bulging stomach, and he was wolfing down a sandwich. When he saw Mark, he waved to him with the remains of his sandwich. "Have something to eat!" he said. "You must be hungry. Never saw a boy who wasn't." He laughed loudly, a hoarse, barking laugh, as though he had said something funny.

Mark nodded and went over to the table, trying not to look at the bit of mayonnaise that was clinging to the side of the man's mouth. But the man had given Mark just the opportunity he needed. Mark took two sandwiches, but he didn't eat them. Instead, he took them to his room and closed the door. Then he got out the knapsack that he and Pete had brought with them and put the sandwiches in that. Looking around the room, he saw Pete's sneakers, and he put them in the knapsack, too.

He waited for a while, then opened his door a crack and looked into the kitchen. The fat man was gone now. Mark went and took three more sandwiches, brought them back to his room, and put them in the knapsack with the others. Then, waiting until no one was in the kitchen or on the porch, he quietly slipped out, holding the knapsack in front of him, trying to shield it with his body. He walked casually, as though he were just looking around the house. When he was out of sight of the building, he put the knapsack on his shoulders, threading his arms through the straps.

He knew exactly what he was going to do. He would begin the way he had this morning. He'd go down to Eric's house along the path, then back to the lake again, walking near the path, but off into the woods. He would go up and back, each time going a little deeper into the woods. He was looking for Pete, but he was looking for something else too: he was looking for the thick underbrush, the hidden, silent places where a deer could hide. He knew Pete. Pete was out there somewhere. And there were deer out there, too. If there were deer, Pete would find them. All Mark had to do was find the deer, and he would find his brother.

Not running this time, Mark walked quietly and deliberately through the woods. Every hundred feet or so, he stopped and called softly, "Pete? Pe-ete!" He listened for an answer, then went on.

He reached Eric's house and stopped, looking around carefully. He would ask Eric once more if Pete had been by. There wasn't anything to hide anymore, and it was possible that Pete had come back to see the deer. Mark went up to the door and knocked.

"Hello!" Eric said when he opened the door. "Did you find him? I saw some people . . ." Noticing the look on Mark's face, he stopped, then added, "You didn't find him, did you?"

Mark shook his head. "I was hoping you'd seen him."

"I'm sorry." Eric had his glasses in his hand, and he chewed on the frame, his eyes squinting, as though he were deep in thought. "Who are the men who passed before?"

"Volunteer firemen."

Eric settled on the porch railing. "Hmmm. I don't see how your brother could disappear. These woods are big, but not particularly deep."

"They think that maybe he drowned!" Saying it out loud made it seem more real, and Mark had to swallow hard in order not to cry.

Eric looked up quickly, then away. "What do you think?" he asked softly.

"I don't think he drowned. He can swim . . . well."

"You sure?"

"Uh-huh." He was struggling not to cry.

"Then he's in the woods," Eric said matter-of-factly, and the words and the voice suddenly reassured Mark.

"But where?"

Eric looked up at Mark. "Where do you live when you're not here? Would he try to go back home? Who's organizing the search?"

"Dr. Ramirez. I live in town. Aunt Agnes is back at the house, waiting."

"And your parents?"

Again that question. "I don't have any parents!" he blurted out. "What difference does it make?"

"None," Eric said mildly. "Just wondered who was in charge. I think I'll go take a look. I know these woods better than most."

"Can I go with you?" It was on impulse that Mark said that. He wasn't sure he wanted Eric's company, but if the man really knew the woods, well, it was better than looking by himself.

Eric looked Mark up and down, assessing him, but all he finally said was, "Those are lousy shoes."

"It's all right," Mark said. "I don't mind." He knew sneakers weren't much good in the woods, but he hadn't thought to bring heavy shoes with him when he'd left home yesterday.

"I'll see what I can do," Eric said. He disappeared inside the cabin. When he came out, he had a heavy flashlight, a bottle of bug repellent, a canteen, and two pairs of work boots. He handed one pair to Mark. "Try these." He smiled. "They may be too big, but they're better than nothing."

Mark took them. They did look big, but it didn't matter. "Thanks," he said. He sat down on the steps next to Eric and pulled off his sneakers. Silently, quickly, each of them laced up the heavy boots.

X

Mark picked up the flashlight, bug repellent, and canteen and put them into the knapsack. Watching him, Eric smiled. "Looks to me as though you were going to try and find Pete all by yourself."

Mark nodded. "Yeah."

Eric seemed to hesitate before he spoke again. "Does anybody know where you are or what you're doing?"

Mark busied himself with the knapsack, settling it on his shoulders. He didn't look up. "No," he said.

"Well, shouldn't you let somebody know? Isn't there somebody who's going to be worried?"

Mark shook his head, still avoiding Eric's eyes, but his heart was racing. What if Eric wouldn't let him go along?

"You know," Eric continued when Mark didn't reply. "It might not be any of my business, but somebody ought to know where you are. Did you ask if you could go?"

Ask? Mark felt his face get hot. He didn't have to ask permission as if he were a little kid! But Eric was probably right. Dr. Ramirez would have a fit when he discovered that Mark was gone. "Maybe I should have told somebody," he said. "But there's only one person, and he'll know where I am if I'm gone. Besides, it won't take long to find Pete. I know it." Mark glanced up then and hoped his eyes didn't have that pleading look that he felt they had.

"Okay." Eric nodded and turned away. Mark was relieved and even a little surprised. He had expected more of an argument.

They went down the steps, and Eric led the way across the yard, but they had gone only a few hundred feet when he spoke again. "It's okay for now if you come along with me, but I'm not letting you stay out for long. If you appear to be missing, too, you'll be causing lots of problems for those who are looking for Pete."

"I'll go back as soon as we find him," Mark said. He thought he heard Eric mutter something, but he didn't want to know what it was.

Silently, Eric led the way to a path that went through a field and eventually wound into the woods on the far side of the lake. It was a long walk, and they went single-file, Indian fashion, trudging across the open space. Although it was late in the day, the sun was still hot, and it was with relief that Mark saw Eric leave the field and head for a small clump of trees on the far side. In the shade, they stopped to rest for a moment.

Eric wiped his forehead with a handkerchief and stood staring thoughtfully ahead. Mark stared, too, looking into the woods as though he could will his eyes to see through the trees and underbrush. Could Pete really have come this far? Why had they come to search on this side of the lake? Maybe he should have come by himself. Still, Eric said he knew these woods well, and—

"You're thinking something?" Eric was watching him.

"Yes. See, I'm just not sure. I mean, I'm just not sure that Pete could have come this far. I don't know if we should be over here."

"But if everyone else is searching on the far side of the lake, someone is sure to find him there. So we might as well look over here. Unless you have a better idea?"

Mark looked up quickly, not certain whether or not Eric was being sarcastic—grownups so seldom asked advice—but Eric seemed serious. "Well," Mark said slowly. "I'm not sure it's a better idea, but I was thinking about what Pete is like. See, Pete's crazy about animals. So I thought that if we knew where the deer were, then maybe we'd find Pete there."

"Okay," said Eric, "we'll look where the deer are likely to be."

Eric led, heading deep into the woods. He didn't speak again for a long time, but every so often he put out one hand as if he were pointing out something to Mark. Since he never spoke, Mark wasn't sure what it was he was pointing at. Suddenly, Eric held up one hand, a signal for Mark to stop. He pointed.

There, on a fallen tree, was the biggest bird Mark had ever seen. It was about two feet tall, with a crest of red feathers standing straight up in the middle of its head like a bunch of wild hair. It reminded Mark, with a sort of pain, of Pete when he first woke up in the morning. They stood still, watching, until at last, with a huge flapping of its wings, the bird disappeared into the woods.

Eric let out his breath slowly, as if he'd been holding it all that time. He smiled. "Remember that," he said to Mark. "You won't see many pileated woodpeckers. They're rare."

"How do you know it's a pileated woodpecker?" Mark asked.

"It's my job to know," answered Eric.

"It's your job to know birds? What kind of job is that?"

"I'm in wildlife management, at least in the winter. I'm taking the summer off to do some research."

"Oh." Mark nodded. So that was why Eric seemed to know so much about the woods.

They went on silently until the woods closed in around them, thick and dark, the trees tall overhead, the underbrush heavy beneath their feet. An occasional branch hung across the path, and Eric held it back while Mark ducked under. They stopped where the woods were so dense that it seemed they could barely go any farther. It would be a perfect place for deer to hide, but could Pete possibly have come so far?

Careful not to even take a deep breath, Mark looked around. No sign of deer. No sign of Pete. Where *was* Pete? Could he have gone somewhere else, looking for home, maybe, for Grandma? The thought brought a lump to Mark's throat. If only he could read Pete's mind!

Eric interrupted his thoughts by moving close to him and speaking so softly that Mark had to watch his lips to catch the words. "Why don't you call your brother?"

"*Call* him?" Of course! Why hadn't they done it before? Why were they trying so hard to be quiet?

As if Eric had read Mark's mind, he answered softly, "I've thought perhaps that others have been calling Pete, and maybe frightening him. So I thought we'd try it differently by sort of sneaking up on him. But would he answer, do you think?"

Mark laughed, the first genuine relief he had felt all day. "Are you kidding? You heard how Pete shouts!"

Eric laughed, too, and his face softened. "Yeah, I surely did. Go ahead. Call him."

Mark called. "Pete? Pe-ete!"

No answer.

He called again, and then again. He checked his watch. Seven o'clock! It would be dark in little more than an hour.

Eric saw him and nodded in agreement. "There's one more place to search, and then I'm going to take you back home before it's dark."

Mark didn't look up, so his eyes showed nothing, but he was angry. He suppressed what he wanted to say. He was going to stay in these woods as long as he wanted—until his brother was found—and nobody was going to tell him otherwise.

The gathering darkness made the woods seem even denser. Suddenly Mark fell to the ground. A vine was twisted around his foot, and he tore at it. It hurt and he cried out in pain. He tried to scramble to his knees as Eric stopped and came back to him.

"Are you all right?" Eric asked.

Mark nodded. "I just twisted my ankle." He unwrapped the vine and stood up, testing his weight on his foot. "Ow!" He winced. "It's okay," he added quickly.

"We ought to be using the flashlight," Eric said.

Mark took the pack off his back, took out the light, and started to hand it to Eric. But as he stepped forward, he cried out. The pain in his ankle was intense.

Eric came and took the flashlight. He crouched beside Mark. "Let me see your foot," he said.

"No! It's fine!" Mark pulled the foot back, hiding it behind the other one. If Eric knew how much it hurt, he wouldn't let him continue.

"Come on." Eric, still kneeling beside him, looked up. "May I please see your foot?" he said mildly.

"No! Just leave me alone! Let's go."

Eric stood up. "You're not going anywhere," he answered. "I'm going on alone, and when I'm finished, I'll be back. I won't be long. You sit here and rest. There's only one more place I want to look. And you, please, stay here and off that foot."

"I'm not staying here!" Mark answered hotly. "That's my brother who's lost, and I'm finding him, not you."

Eric turned away as if he would go off by himself, but then he stopped. "Look, son . . ." he started to say.

"I'm not your son!" Mark answered. "And stop treating me like a little baby!"

"Then stop acting like one!"

Mark was too surprised to answer.

"I mean it," Eric continued. "I don't know what's eating you, but this isn't a competition to find Pete! We're trying to do this together, aren't we?" He glared at Mark, then continued. "You're only a kid! I don't know how old you are. Twelve? I admire you, trying to get out here and look for your brother. You have a lot of guts! But everybody needs help sometimes, you know. And you're fighting me instead of working with me. You're not helping anybody, least of all yourself. Or Pete!" Eric stopped for breath, his eyes flashing.

Mark looked away. He felt . . . stupid. Words, dumb words, ran around in his brain. "It's not my fault. . . . I'm sorry. . . . Pete's lost. . . . They're going to send him away. . . . It's my fault. . . . I lost him. . . . I shouldn't have run away. . . . Grandma's dead." But no words came out, and he felt tears fill his eyes again.

"Look," Eric said more calmly, putting a hand on Mark's shoulder. "We're in this together, aren't we?"

Mark nodded, unable to speak.

"Okay, now come on. We came out here because we both want to find Pete, and we both think we can. I know something about these woods, and you know something about Pete. Okay?"

Again Mark nodded.

"Okay, how's your foot?"

"It hurts."

"Can you walk on it?"

Mark took a careful step or two, then nodded. It hurt a lot, but he had twisted his ankles much worse than this playing ball. It was bearable.

"Okay then, let's go on together, huh? Partners?"

Mark smiled sheepishly. "Partners," he said.

Eric winked and gave a "thumbs-up" sign.

XI

They went on then, picking their way carefully. The sun was low in the sky, and the slanting rays brought only a little light into the thick woods. It was almost dark, and Eric had already passed something without noticing it when Mark paused, then shouted, "Look! Eric, look!" He snatched a torn piece of cloth from a bush alongside the path. It was small and so dark that it was almost invisible, but Mark instantly recognized it for what it was—a piece of dark blue cloth, a piece of the shirt that Pete had worn yesterday. "Look! He's been here!"

Eric whirled around and held out his hand for the fabric. He held the torn cloth up, trying to see it more clearly in the dim light. "It's new, not faded. It hasn't been here long."

"It's Pete's shirt!"

"Are you sure?"

"Yes, I'm sure! It's the one he was wearing yesterday. I remember because I helped him get dressed yesterday morning. I know it."

"Then he's here. Or he was here."

They stood together silently, hardly daring to breathe, every sense tuned in an effort to detect something—a sound, a movement. They stared at each other as if some secret could be detected by looking into each other's face. Eric spoke first. "It's so very still. I don't think he's here anymore. If he were, we'd hear something."

"Then let's hurry and catch up with him."

"Call him, just in case."

"Pete?" Mark called. "Peter?"

An echo came back, but nothing more.

"Pete! Pete? It's me, Mark! Can you hear me?"

Only silence. It was Eric who saw something this time. He touched Mark's arm and pointed silently.

In the bushes in front of them something stirred. Just one branch wavered back and forth, but it swayed so distinctly, without any breeze to disturb it, that something else had to be moving it. "Pete?" Mark called again, and for some reason, his voice was shaking. "Pete, if that's you, come out."

Very, very slowly, Eric stepped toward the bush. Instantly, there was a crash in the underbrush and the sound of footsteps running. But whoever or whatever was there was not running toward them, but rather running away.

As if propelled by a cannon, Mark and Eric shot forward. The crashing went on, and they followed headlong, tumbling forward, thrusting branches aside, pounding ahead. "Pete! Peter, don't go! It's me!" Mark shouted, almost in tears. They were so close. Pete mustn't run away now.

But then Mark had to pause. The pain in his ankle was almost unbearable. At that moment he and Eric both noticed that the sound—the running up ahead —had stopped.

"What happened?" Mark cried out.

"I don't know!" Eric stood still, listening.

"Where are you, Pete?" Mark listened, then called again, softly, "Pete?"

Only the cry of a bird broke the silence.

"He has to be there," Eric said rapidly and very quietly. "He must be just up ahead, maybe even in the bushes, watching us."

"But why would he do that?" Mark was close to tears. "That's not like Pete."

"He's frightened. Maybe afraid of me. Can you go ahead alone?"

Go alone? Memories came back to him of people who said they had seen bears in the woods.

"It's not an animal," Eric said, as though he had had a similar thought. "Animals don't act that way." He handed the flashlight to Mark. "Can you do it?"

Mark nodded. He took the flashlight and walked forward, limping slightly. His heart was pounding hard, making a thunderous sound, threatening to overwhelm him. One step, two steps. Pretend something. Think about something else. He was a little boy again, playing a game: "May I take one giant step?" "Yes, you may take one giant step." Three giant steps. Ten giant steps. Why was he afraid? It was only his brother, wasn't it?

He was many steps from Eric now, and he looked back over his shoulder. He could just see the faint gleam of Eric's plaid shirt in the dusk. He turned back to the path. Then his pounding heart leaped, and joy spread through him. He knew instantly that he would never feel quite this way again. There on the path in front of Mark—his eyes squeezed shut, his arms outstretched, fat tears running down his round little cheeks—was Pete.

Mark reached out, and Pete tumbled into his outstretched arms. They hugged, rocking back and forth, and Mark was not quite sure who was comforting whom. Hot, salty tears ran down his face, but he wasn't sure whether they were his or Pete's. He knew only that Pete was here, safe, and he'd never let his brother go again.

Pete's chest was heaving with sobs, but no sound came out. He was torn and scratched, his shirt hanging in tatters, mud mingling with his tears.

"Pete," Mark whispered. "Pete, it's all right."

"Unhhh!" A sound tore out of Pete's throat, a not quite human sound, like that of a wild animal in pain.

"It's all right. It's all right. It really is. I found you." Mark laughed then, relief making him almost hysterical. "I mean, *you* found me!" Pete's arms were wound around Mark so tightly that Mark's chest began to hurt, but he didn't pull away. "It's all right, all right," he said soothingly.

Pete began to cry loudly. "Gone!" he wailed suddenly. "Lost!"

"I know. I know," Mark whispered.

"Lost!" Pete shouted again, accusingly.

"I know, Pete. I know just how you feel. Once when I was really little, maybe even before you were born, I got lost, too." The words tumbled out, as Mark recalled a memory he had hardly known he had until this moment. "We went on a picnic or somewhere, and I got lost going to the bathroom. And, Pete, I was really scared. But it's okay now."

"No!" Pete shouted.

Mark began to laugh. The same old Pete. "No what?" Mark asked. He pulled himself loose from Pete's grip, but he kept patting his brother's face gently, affectionately. "I brought you food," he said softly.

Immediately, Pete stopped sobbing, but he got a strange, wary expression on his face. He glanced over Mark's shoulder, as though he were looking in Eric's direction. Eric! Mark had almost forgotten about him. He turned around, but there was no sign of Eric coming along behind. He must have decided to wait where he was. Pete was poking at Mark, reaching for food.

Mark took the knapsack off, dug around in it, and found the sandwiches. He hadn't wrapped them before he left, and they were kind of stiff now, but he knew Pete would be too hungry for that to matter much. He handed a sandwich to Pete. Instead of gobbling it as Mark had expected, Pete put the sandwich behind his back. He took several steps backward away from Mark.

"Pete?"

"What?"

"What are you doing?"

"Nothing." He backed up a little farther.

"Pete, come on!" Mark was puzzled. "What are you up to?"

Pete shook his head. Then he turned around—his back to Mark, his arms folded—standing the way he did when he was being stubborn.

"Pete, what are you doing? Will you cut it out?"

"Promise!" Pete demanded.

"Promise? Promise what? I don't even know what you're talking about."

"Promise!" Pete insisted, and he shouted it this time.

"I promise. Okay? But I don't have any idea what I'm promising. Okay?"

"Okay." Grudgingly.

"Now what is it?"

"Here." Pete took Mark's sleeve with just two fingers and began pulling him away from the trail and deeper into the underbrush. Nervously, Mark looked over his shoulder. Where was Eric? Pete was leading him on, tugging at him as a small child might. They didn't go far, only about a couple dozen steps from where Pete had first appeared on the path, but the underbrush was so dense that even the beam of the flashlight barely penetrated it. "Hush!" Pete put one finger over his lips, the way Grandma had done to him so often. "Hush!" he warned Mark.

Mark nodded, suddenly aware in some dim corner of his mind that the roles seemed to be reversed, and Pete was the one in charge. And then Pete was kneeling, holding the sandwich outstretched. In front of him in the bushes was a deer—a tiny, spotted baby deer! For a minute, Mark could hardly take it in. A deer, just lying on the ground, not making any attempt to flee? But it was quivering with fear. "Pete. Oh, Pete, how did you . . . ?"

And then Mark saw why Pete's shirt was all torn up. He had ripped it into narrow strips and made a bandage of it, wrapping it around the deer's leg. It was lumpy and awkward-looking, but it was definitely a bandage. How had Pete known what to do? Then Mark remembered suddenly how Dr. Ramirez had once bandaged one of the many hurt animals that Pete had found—a rabbit whose leg had been caught in a trap. But this shirt bandage was now soaked with blood. Had the deer been shot—by the poachers, perhaps? It was too much to take in all at once, especially because Eric appeared then. Silently, without even a crackle of the branches underfoot, he had appeared beside them. And when he did, Pete began to cry. "It's *my* deer!" he shouted at Eric. "Mine!"

No one replied.

"Mine!" Pete cried again. He stood up, putting his body between Eric and the deer, as though he were shielding it. "Mine!" Tears began running down his face again.

Slowly something began coming clear to Mark. He didn't know yet how Pete had gotten here. He didn't know yet what had happened to the deer or how Pete had found it. But he understood now why Pete had been running and hiding. He was hiding from Eric because he had seen Eric with the deer yesterday—maybe even thought they belonged to him—and was afraid Eric would take this one away.

Eric must have understood at the same time because he said quietly, "It's all right Pete. She's *your* deer, not mine."

"You can't have her!" Pete insisted again.

"I don't want her, Pete. She's your deer."

"Promise!"

Mark laughed out loud at Pete's insistence, but Eric answered seriously, "I promise."

Pete took a deep breath, bent over, and gathered the deer into his arms. He struggled to stand up, cradling the fawn close to his chest. Mark reached out a hand to steady him. When Pete was finally on his feet, the animal in his arms almost overwhelmed him. When it had been lying on the ground, it had appeared small. Now, in Pete's arms, it was as big as a fair-sized dog, and its legs dangled down, almost reaching the ground. But Pete seemed undaunted. "Go home," he said simply.

Eric and Mark exchanged a look and then a smile. "Let's go home," Eric said.

The sun had long since set by the time they were out of the woods and had come to the path that led around the lake to the cabin. Mark had had to stop to rest his ankle frequently, and Pete had to rest with the fawn. He hadn't let anyone else carry it, and although it must have been very heavy for him, neither Mark nor Eric had tried to take it away.

As they reached the clearing that led to the cabin, Mark could see that every light inside was lit and searchlights had been set up at the dock, although no one was outside. For one brief moment Mark felt something like panic, the same kind of feeling he'd had when Dr. Ramirez first arrived this morning. Was it only this morning? He felt he should turn and run, but they were already on the path. Mark took a deep breath and put one hand on Pete's shoulder. Eric opened the door of the cabin.

For a moment, everything stood still. Everyone inside—those talking or eating or just standing—stopped, staring. Aunt Agnes was at the table. Why was she here now? She turned, her face uncomprehending, and then her eyes widened and one hand flew up to her mouth. Dr. Ramirez was pouring coffee, and he stopped, the coffeepot in midair.

Suddenly, as if everyone had just been released from a trance, things happened. People began talking, laughing. Aunt Agnes ran across the room and grabbed Mark, squeezing him harder than even Pete had done. Then she released him and turned to Pete.

Dr. Ramirez held Mark next, ran his hands over

Mark's face and arms and legs as though he were feeling for broken bones. But somehow Mark knew that the doctor was really trying to reassure himself that Mark was really there. Dr. Ramirez didn't speak, though, and there were tears in his eyes. He turned from Mark, and then he, too, went to Pete.

Mark let someone lead him to a table, and he sat down. He knew someone handed him something to drink, and he tried to say thank you, but no words came out. He looked across the room—at Pete—at Eric—at the deer. Then, he folded his arms on the table and put his head down. In an instant, he was asleep.

XII

When Mark woke, sunlight was streaming
through the bedroom windows, lying in big square
patches on his bed and on the bare floor. As he lay
halfway between sleep and wakefulness, he was
aware of being sore and stiff, but very, very happy.
Why happy? he wondered as he drifted to sleep
again. It was a dream, surely, of himself and Pete
and a deer. A deer was bounding through the forest,
and Pete was chasing it, shouting, *"My* deer! *Mine!"*
And then Mark was wide awake, and it wasn't a
dream at all. He remembered yesterday clearly—
Pete lost and the woods and the deer and everybody
out searching.

He closed his eyes again. He would go back to
sleep. Aunt Agnes was there to take care of Pete,
and Dr. Ramirez was probably there, too. Oh, man!
He sat up suddenly, thoughts tumbling about in his

brain like a storm. Aunt Agnes! Dr. Ramirez! They must be mad at him for taking Pete away and letting him get lost! And what was Aunt Agnes going to do now that they had been found? Would she send Pete away? No! He'd run away again if he had to. Then a voice, hiding somewhere in the back of his head, mocked him: "Sure. Good idea. Run away and get lost again?"

"Shut up!" he told himself out loud. He looked over to Pete's bed, but Pete was gone already, probably out with the deer. Well, he was Aunt Agnes's problem now. Mark swung his legs over the side of the bed, stood up, and the pain shot from his ankle almost up to his knee. *That* was no dream! He limped over to the dresser, got out jeans and a shirt, and put them on. He might as well go out and face them now. Stepping carefully, he went to the bed-room door, opened it, and looked into the kitchen. Aunt Agnes and Dr. Ramirez were at the table, talking softly.

Looking at Aunt Agnes, Mark was startled. From a certain angle, she looked so much like Grandma. For a moment, neither Aunt Agnes nor Dr. Ramirez realized that Mark stood there. Then they both seemed to see him at the same time, and Aunt Agnes got up. "Mark, come here," she said, pointing to a place beside her. She went to the stove, came back with a steaming pot, and began ladling something that looked like stew into a plate. "You need some food in that stomach, and not a word out of you until it's all finished." She seemed perfectly matter-of-fact, the way she was any other time, worrying about whether or not he ate well.

Mark went over, stepping carefully on his sore leg, and sat down, his heart thumping hard. He was sure he wouldn't be able to eat a thing, but after the first mouthful, he realized he was starved. It was weird, stew for breakfast, but it was good, too, and he was glad to eat and not say anything.

Dr. Ramirez and Aunt Agnes watched for a while, and then Dr. Ramirez spoke. "You did quite a job last night," he said.

Mark looked up, trying to tell by the expression on the doctor's face what was meant by "quite a job," but he couldn't.

"How did you know where Pete might be? Eric says you suggested looking for the deer. That was good thinking."

"I told you not to say a word until he's eaten everything on his plate!" Aunt Agnes interrupted.

Dr. Ramirez gave her a quizzical look, then he winked at Mark.

Aunt Agnes saw the wink. "Well, you can *talk* all you want," she added sharply. "Just don't ask him questions." She smiled at Dr. Ramirez then, as if to soften what she had just said.

Dr. Ramirez winked at her this time, and she laughed out loud.

Watching them, Mark was surprised. They seemed so, well, so *normal*, fooling a little, but not angry. How come? Because he was sure to be in a lot of trouble.

Nobody spoke again until Mark finished, and then he was the one who spoke first. Without glancing up, he said, "I guess you're pretty mad at me."

No one answered.

"Well, are you?" He looked at Aunt Agnes. "I mean, I don't blame you. I lost Pete."

Aunt Agnes opened her mouth to speak, then closed it again. Mark saw her exchange a look with

Dr. Ramirez. What had they been talking about?

Suddenly, he was tired of secrets, tired of adults keeping secrets about him and Pete from him, of his keeping secrets from everybody else. "This isn't fair!" he burst out. "All these decisions about Pete and me and not telling me. . . ." He looked at Dr. Ramirez. "You, too!" he said.

The doctor nodded, then turned to the window and seemed to be staring intently at the lake. There was a long silence, broken by Aunt Agnes. "Why don't you trust me?" she blurted out.

"Trust you?"

"Yes, trust me!" Her voice was shaking. "You won't even let me near you. You won't let me near Pete. You sneak off in the middle of the night. Why? What did I ever do to you?"

What did she ever do? The words he had heard, that he would never forget, ran through his brain again. "Pete . . . special school . . . away . . . not much money . . ."

His heart beat faster. "You're going to put Pete in an institution! Lock him up like some kind of—of animal! Pete wouldn't do that, not to anyone! Not even to an animal!" He was crying suddenly. "He's not stupid! I bet he knows what you're up to. He's my *brother*!"

"I know that!" Aunt Agnes sat straight up in her chair, her hands clasped tightly together. She was folding and unfolding them as though she were trying to hold onto something that was about to escape her. "Mark, nobody wants to do this! We've been sitting up all night talking about it. You need to have a life of your own. Pete needs a school." She paused then. "I know you overheard us talking. Dr. Ramirez told me about it, and I'm really sorry. But don't you see that I can't watch Pete all the time? Didn't you see—didn't you prove to yourself—that he has to be watched every minute?" She stopped, unfolded her hands, then folded them tightly again. She looked at him, her eyes shiny, as though she were about to cry. "What would *you* do? What do *you* think is right?"

"Not an institution! It's a . . . cage!"

"It isn't! You don't understand! We're talking about a school. . . ." She broke off, and her face had a squeezed look.

Dr. Ramirez reached across the table and patted her clenched hands. He turned to Mark. "Mark, you said it yourself. Pete's no dummy. He has certain problems. His brain doesn't work like ours. But he's not stupid. He has a right to training and learning and a life of his own."

"He *has* a life of his own!" Mark answered.

"Mark?" Dr. Ramirez's voice was calm and soft. "What do you want to do with Pete? What would you choose if you had to make the decision?"

Mark looked from Dr. Ramirez to Aunt Agnes. Her eyes were still shiny. "She shouldn't cry," he thought.

What would he choose? He could take Pete away again, take him to the city as he had planned. Then the voice in the back of his head mocked him again. "You could lose Pete again. In a big city it would be exciting."

He was aware at that moment of the silence inside and the noises outside—a hammering, a gentle licking sound of the waves on the lake, a mockingbird singing. What would he do if the decision were his?

He looked up at the doctor. Dr. Ramirez had shaved since yesterday, but his face still had a tired, drawn look. "Why, he's old, too," Mark thought suddenly! "He's old and he's tired, and he doesn't know what to do either."

Mark glanced down at his own hands in his lap, then up at the two of them. "I don't know what's right to do," he answered slowly, honestly. "I just don't know."

"Then can we at least talk about it?" Dr. Ramirez asked. "Shall we examine the options and see what would be acceptable to everybody and good for Pete?"

Mark started to nod agreement and suddenly realized what he was agreeing to—that he would *consider* letting Pete go to school. But he knew then that he hadn't just made that decision, that he had really made it yesterday in the woods when he realized that Pete had to be watched every second.

Before he could answer, Dr. Ramirez spoke, as though heading off any objections Mark might have. "Mark," he said, leaning across the table, "have you ever been to a school for kids like Pete?"

"Once. That time Grandma sent him."

"That wasn't a proper school," Dr. Ramirez answered. "It was one of the many experiments they tried when they were learning to teach kids with problems. No, I mean a school especially for kids like Pete."

"No, I guess not."

"Would you like to see one?"

"I don't know."

"Just come with me once. I think you'll be pleased when you see what it can do for kids like Pete."

"Can Pete see it too?"

"Of course."

"But we're not sending him away?" Mark's heart

began racing wildly again. "I mean, *we're not sending him away* from home." What could he do about it if they insisted?

"No," Dr. Ramirez answered. "We're not going to send him away. And Aunt Agnes and I feel really bad about trying to make such an important decision without consulting you. We—well, we had some difficult decisions to make too, and adults don't always know what's best, either."

"Do *you* want to send him away?" Mark turned to Aunt Agnes.

"No. Not away."

Mark felt a huge swelling of relief inside him, of victory. He had won! He had really won! Pete would be with him always. A part of him wanted to jump up quickly and leave before they could change their minds. Another part wanted one last reassurance. The part that needed to be reassured won. "Are you sure? Do you promise?"

Again, Dr. Ramirez and Aunt Agnes exchanged looks. "As far as we can promise, we promise," Aunt Agnes said slowly, and Dr. Ramirez nodded agreement.

"Okay," Mark whispered. It wasn't a perfect promise, but it was a promise. He stood up. "Where's Pete?"

Aunt Agnes smiled. "Outside with Eric and the deer. They're building a pen and a bed!"

Mark went out to the porch, trying not to limp, not wanting the doctor to fuss over him. He felt stunned, happy, and confused. What about Grandma? What would she think? Would it be all right with her? He looked down at the dock where Pete and Eric were busy working. "Hi, Pete!" he called.

Pete looked up. "Come!" he ordered.

Eric wiped his forehead with the back of one hand. "Some people sleep all day, and others have been working for hours," he said, grinning.

Mark grinned too. He went down the steps and inspected the contraption they were building. There were two boxes, one with straw and grass lining it, and a bigger one, still under construction, that looked like a pen. In the smaller of the boxes was the fawn, its leg expertly bandaged now. Mark bent and touched her, one hand resting lightly on her warm back. She quivered slightly at the touch but didn't try to move away. How beautiful she was!

Pete moved in in front of Mark but didn't push him away. Mark smiled, realizing that Pete was acting protective as a mother deer might.

Mark punched Pete's arm lightly, then stood up and turned to Eric. "That's quite a thing you're building."

"I'm getting lots of help," Eric answered. "Just like yesterday. Partners." He smiled.

Mark smiled back, then left them and walked slowly back up to the house. There was so much to think about—Pete, school. What would Grandma think? Would she be angry at him, disappointed in him? It had been so important to her to keep Pete with her. But right now Mark was happy, and Pete was happy. His brother was safe and sound, and he had his deer. A deer! Just what they needed. One more thing to watch, one more problem! Who would take care of the deer while Pete was at school? Who was taking care of the deer now? Who was taking care of Pete, making sure that he didn't disappear again? And suddenly Mark stopped, surprised, because for the first time in a long time there were answers, and it felt as though his world was coming back into shape again. Aunt Agnes was taking care of Pete. Eric would look after the fawn. And Mark? His ankle still hurt, and he thought now he'd ask Dr. Ramirez to check it. He smiled then. Someone to care for Pete. Someone to look after the fawn. Someone to help him. Suddenly, he was very, very happy not to be doing it all alone.

XIII

The next few weeks were a series of almost dreamlike days—of sunning, fishing, swimming, and resting—the first vacation Mark had had all summer. But then as the season drew to a close, the days took on a nightmarish quality as Mark thought of Pete starting school. Inevitably, though, the day came when they had to move back to town. Dr. Ramirez drove out to the lake to pick up Aunt Agnes and Pete and Mark, and the first thing they did was to go to the school Dr. Ramirez and Aunt Agnes had chosen for Pete.

As they drove up in front of the school, Mark looked around carefully at the playground, the parking lots, the building itself, trying to find something wrong with it. Yet it was just a school, very much like any other school, except that maybe it was prettier. The playground was big, with swings and lots of other equipment; and in one corner of the yard was a penned-in place where there were ducks and rabbits. Pete sat down with a rabbit and didn't move again until a teacher came and took him by the hand to show him around.

Aunt Agnes, Dr. Ramirez, and Mark talked to the teachers and went to the classrooms. The rooms were big and sunny, with books and desks and chairs, much like regular classrooms, but in one corner of each room was a carpeted place with toys and building blocks. Finally, at the end of the visit, Mark felt good. This school might really work out well for Pete. He was glad he had agreed to consider the idea. Now, Pete would begin school next week, just like everybody else.

Early on the first day of school, Mark stood with Aunt Agnes and Pete by the gate, waiting for the buses that would take each boy to his own school. Mark kept sneaking looks at Pete to see whether he seemed scared, but Pete looked the way he usually did. He pointed and watched silently as a squirrel scampered along a fence across the road, and Aunt Agnes had to hold his hand tightly to keep him from running over. Mark was grateful that Pete's bus came first. Pete climbed on, shouting "Good-bye!" at the top of his lungs, and although Mark searched his face, he couldn't see any sign of fear.

Mark was scared, though. The entire day he couldn't pay attention to anything. He twisted around in his seat and stared out the window, his mind far away with Pete. Once, his teacher, Miss Burke, appeared beside him, staring at him as though waiting for an answer, and he realized he hadn't heard a word she'd said. She bent over him and tapped him smartly on the head. "You've had too much summer vacation," she said. As she bent over him, he winced and immediately named her "Bad Breath Burke." At last, though, the day was over, and he raced home from the bus stop. As he ran toward the porch, he saw Pete sitting on the steps, a small, bluntish knife in his hand.

"Peter!" Mark yelled. He reached down, about to snatch the knife from Pete. Pete should never have a knife. He would . . . and then Mark stopped when he saw what Pete was doing. His brother held a small block of wood in one hand and was carving a deer— small, awkward-looking, but definitely a deer. "Who made that?" Mark demanded, fear and worry making him sound angry.

"Me." Pete didn't look up.

"You?"

"Me."

"Really?"

Pete didn't reply.

Slowly Mark sank down on the step beside Pete. He punched him lightly, hoping Pete would look up so he could tell by the expression on his brother's face how the day had gone. But Pete was absorbed in his carving. "Well?" Mark said at last. "How was school? What'd you do?"

"Nothing."

"Nothing? Well, what was it like? Did you like it?"

Pete shrugged.

"Uh . . . did you miss me?"

"No."

Mark couldn't help laughing. Then, although he kept pestering Pete with questions about his day, Pete seemed much more interested in his carving than in talking. He only shrugged in response to Mark's questions.

It went on that way for a week. Always when Mark came home from school, Pete was sitting on the steps, frowning with concentration over his carvings—and by then, he had created almost an entire tiny zoo. One day Mark plopped down beside Pete on the step and asked the usual question, "How was your day."

Pete looked up then. "Bor*ing*!" he shouted, but his voice sounded funny, as though he were about to laugh.

Boring? Mark had never heard Pete use that word before.

"Tommy said so," Pete added, still shouting.

"Who's Tommy?"

"My friend. 'Teacher's a cow,' Tommy said. Bor-*ing*!" Pete was shouting and grinning.

"Shush, Pete!" But Mark laughed, too. "Sounds like my school. Pete, what are you carving today?"

Pete bent over his carving again and didn't bother to answer.

"Pete?"

Still he didn't reply.

"Come on, Pete! What are you making?"

Pete looked up, holding the little unfinished animal in his hand. "Teacher says somebody's busy . . . *leave him alone*!" He shouted that part of it.

Mark shook his head. Pete seemed so different lately. From just one week at school? But there *was* something different. Mark continued to watch him quietly, not daring to disturb him now, but trying to determine what made him seem so changed. What was it?

"Mark?" Aunt Agnes came out on the porch, a

tray of brownies and two glasses of milk in her hands. "How was your day?"

Mark got up, but before he could answer, Pete shouted, "Bor*ing*!"

Aunt Agnes put the snack on the steps between them, then went to the porch swing and patted the place alongside her. "Sit with me for a minute."

Mark took his brownies and sat down, remembering what it was like when Grandma was here, how they used to sit out here after school and talk about the day. But he kept watching Pete, frowning at him slightly.

"What are you thinking?" Aunt Agnes asked.

"About Pete. He seems—different. I can't figure it out."

Aunt Agnes nodded, agreeing.

They were both quiet for a while, watching Pete with his knife, intent on his tiny figure.

"Tommy says . . ." Pete said suddenly in a loud voice.

"Tommy? Who's this Tommy?"

But Pete didn't answer. He only shook his head and then stuck his tongue between his teeth, concentrating on his work again.

Tommy? Boring? A knife with which to carve? Slowly Mark began to realize what was different about Pete. Pete was talking about things, doing things that Mark didn't know anything about. Pete had something all his own, apart from Mark. And it was the first time in his life that that had happened.

Mark blinked in wonder as a whole new train of thought ran though his mind. What did Mark have that was all his own? All his life, he had stayed with Pete, come home right after school so Pete would have someone to play with. He remembered that day early in the summer and how bored he'd been. He couldn't think of even one friend he might play with. He hadn't realized until this minute how much he had missed playing with friends, having some time to himself—things everybody else had. He stood up slowly, taking his plate and glass with him. "I'll put these inside," he said to Aunt Agnes. "I have to change."

Aunt Agnes nodded, and Mark went into the house. But he did not go straight to his room. Instead, he went down the hall to Aunt Agnes's room, the one that used to belong to Grandma. There was a picture of Grandma on the dresser, and he picked it up and carried it to the window to see it better. He looked at it for a long time, trying to remember, to get a feeling again of what Grandma was *really* like, not just in a picture. He remembered that day by the porch when he had looked up and seen her watching him. "You are a very nice person," she said that day. "A very, very nice person." And he remembered how he had said, "You're pretty nice, too." He swallowed hard. "Grandma," he whispered to her. "Don't be mad at me for saying this, but I think you made a mistake about Pete and school and about me, too. I mean, I think you did just about everything else right, but this time—this one thing —you were wrong. See, Pete seems happier now. He has somebody to care for him besides you and me and Aunt Agnes. I love him, and I'll care for him always. But you know what? It's time for me, too, isn't it? And I still love you. Maybe, I even love you more." He put the picture back on the dresser and turned to the door, tears blurring his eyes.

He went to his room and changed, went back to the porch and stood there looking down at Pete. His brother was still intent on his work. Mark frowned. He wanted to leave, to go find somebody to play with, to talk to, but he didn't know whom yet. But somebody besides Pete. "Hey, Pete?" he said. "I'm going off for a while, but I'll be back soon. Okay?"

Pete didn't answer.

"Pete?"

"Hold your—shirt on!" Pete yelled.

"Pete, shush!" Mark said. "Listen, I'll be back soon. Okay?"

Pete looked up. "Okay," he said simply, and he didn't shout it.

"Okay!" Mark jumped down from the steps and ran out of the yard. He stopped and locked the gate behind him, then turned and looked back. Pete was still busy with his carving, something all his own. Mark turned then to the road to go—where? He wasn't sure yet. But to something—something all his own.

DISCARD